No More Fighting

NO MORE FIGHTING

20 MINUTES
A WEEK *to a* STRONGER
RELATIONSHIP

ALICIA MUÑOZ, LPC

Foreword by Dr. Tammy Nelson

ZEPHYROS
PRESS

For general information on our other products and services or to obtain technical support, please contact our Customer Care Department within the US at (866) 744-2665, or outside the US at (510) 253-0500.

Zephyros Press publishes its books in a variety of electronic and print formats. Some content that appears in print may not be available in electronic books, and vice versa.

Interior Designer: Jennifer Durrant
Cover Designer: Katy Brown
Editor: Pippa White
Production Editor: Erum Khan

ISBN: Print 978-1-64152-182-6 | eBook 978-1-64152-183-3

TO CAROL KRAMER SLEPIAN,
for inspiring, healing, and leading
through your passion for Imago,
and for giving me the keys to life and love.

CONTENTS

Foreword   xiii

Introduction   xv

Self-Care

CHAPTER 1   The Oxygen Mask   2

CHAPTER 2   Saying No   6

STEPPING STONE   Self-Care   10

Communication

CHAPTER 3   Feeling Your Feelings   12

CHAPTER 4   The Stories We Tell Ourselves   16

CHAPTER 5   Listening   20

STEPPING STONE   Communication Stoppers   24

Your Partner's World

CHAPTER 6   Validation   26

CHAPTER 7   Empathy   29

STEPPING STONE   The Imago Dialogue   32

Intimacy Issues

CHAPTER 8   Intimacy Tolerance   34

CHAPTER 9   Vulnerability   38

STEPPING STONE   Intimacy Comfort Levels   42

Taking Responsibility

CHAPTER 10   You Should Know What I Need   44

CHAPTER 11   Psychological Ownership   48

CHAPTER 12   Projection   52

STEPPING STONE   Vent Boxes   55

Love Rituals

CHAPTER 13   Check-Ins   57

CHAPTER 14   Takeoffs and Reentries   61

CHAPTER 15   Appreciations and Gratitude   65

STEPPING STONE   Tandem Emotional Mountain Climbing   69

Self-Esteem

CHAPTER 16   Inferiority and Superiority   71

CHAPTER 17   Reparenting Your Own Inner Orphan   75

STEPPING STONE   The Huddle   79

Life Philosophy

CHAPTER 18   Different Values   81

CHAPTER 19   Scarcity and Abundance   85

STEPPING STONE   Infinite Universes   89

Social Styles

CHAPTER 20   Extrovert, Introvert, or Ambivert   91

CHAPTER 21   Relationships with Friends   95

STEPPING STONE   What You Need to Receive, I Need to Give   99

Attachment Issues

CHAPTER 22   Excessive Dependence   101

CHAPTER 23   Counterdependency   105

CHAPTER 24   Unconditional Love   109

STEPPING STONE   Messengers in Disguise   114

Power and Control

CHAPTER 25   Gender Roles and Relationship Roles   116

CHAPTER 26   Shared Decision-Making   120

STEPPING STONE   Compare and Despair   124

Ruptures

CHAPTER 27   The Damage of Disrespect   126

CHAPTER 28   Expressing Anger   130

CHAPTER 29   Understanding Your Triggers   134

STEPPING STONE   What to Do Mid-Fight   138

The Art of Repair

CHAPTER 30   Being *Right* or Being *in Relationship*   141

CHAPTER 31   Remorse and Forgiveness   145

STEPPING STONE   Sensation Is Information   148

Money Matters

CHAPTER 32   The Meaning of Money   150

CHAPTER 33   My Money, Your Money, Our Money   154

STEPPING STONE   Time Management   158

Coping with Stress

CHAPTER 34   Different Kinds of Stress   160

CHAPTER 35   Fight, Flight, or Freeze   164

STEPPING STONE   From Distress to Eustress   169

Parenting

CHAPTER 36   Parenting Styles   171

CHAPTER 37   Blended Family   175

CHAPTER 38   In-Laws   179

STEPPING STONE   Move It   184

Love Languages

CHAPTER 39 Identifying Your Love Language 186

CHAPTER 40 Speaking Your Partner's Love Language 189

CHAPTER 41 To-Do Love Lists 192

STEPPING STONE It's Already Happening 196

Sexuality

CHAPTER 42 Desire Discrepancy 198

CHAPTER 43 Understanding Sexual Shame 203

CHAPTER 44 Erotic Blueprints 208

STEPPING STONE What's in a Word? 212

Relationship Wreckers

CHAPTER 45 Addictions 214

CHAPTER 46 Dishonesty 218

CHAPTER 47 Wanting What We Don't Have 222

STEPPING STONE Radical Honesty Shares 226

Monogamy and Beyond

CHAPTER 48   Affairs   229

CHAPTER 49   Resilient Monogamy   232

CHAPTER 50   Polyamory   238

STEPPING STONE   Being "All-In"   243

General Inspiration

CHAPTER 51   Loving Imperfectly   245

CHAPTER 52   Celebrating Life Together   249

STEPPING STONE   Sustainable Love   253

Resources and References   255

Online Articles and Websites   257

Index   259

Foreword

Alicia Muñoz is one of those special people. She is destined to change the way we relate to one another. She's a couple's therapist with a passion for growth, depth, and authenticity. She is also someone who you just know is meant to take us all into the next dimension, where pleasure and connection are the measures by which we judge our lives. In this book, she uses her own experiences and those of her clients to motivate and inspire readers to strengthen their bond in a sustainable way in romantic relationships. It's a book that can help us all.

I am a certified sex and couples therapist, an author, and a wife. And if I am honest—as honest as Muñoz encourages us to be with ourselves and one another—I do not have a perfect marriage. Everyone always asks my husband about his wife, the sex therapist, at parties: "So, you must have a great time with your wife!" And most times, he answers with a smile and a wink, "Oh, you have no idea . . ." And for the most part, we do have a great relationship, we resolve our conflicts well, and we adore one another. But we do not have a perfect marriage, because there's no such thing.

That is why I love this book. Between the first chapter, "The Oxygen Mask," and the final chapters, "Loving Imperfectly" and "Celebrating Life Together," Muñoz takes readers on an intimate journey through the lives of relatable couples who are learning to enjoy their own messy imperfections, embrace being human together, and overcome the common challenges couples face. It can be done, and she shows us how. This is wonderful, because there are times when I, too, struggle to find a way to celebrate my partner, even though I love him and I've been working with couples for almost 30 years. Marriage is hard.

When couples fight, it can feel like a tropical storm. Reactivity can bring down lines of communication and leave obstacles behind that block connection. If you are in a relationship where your arguments escalate, you know that fights can come on unpredictably, and strong. The frustration of arguing with your partner can leave you feeling hopeless over time. It's defeating. Without a connection to the intimacy that brought you together, a relationship can feel empty and really, really lonely.

In this book, Muñoz focuses on helping couples develop "antifragility," which she discusses in her chapter on "Resilient Monogamy." This concept is similar to my work in *The New Monogamy*. Couples can clear away debris left behind by fights and reestablish lines of communication after a crisis. It's even possible to learn how to maintain intimacy when 80-mile-an-hour winds are blowing through your relational lives. With engaging stories and once-weekly doable exercises, Muñoz offers readers a system for working together outside of a therapist's office. Many of the issues that crop up in relationships can be healed through this book. Caring can become a weekly practice.

If you want to create a relationship where you are both "all in," this book is for you. Anyone looking to be inspired can learn to love and to celebrate life together. Alicia Muñoz teaches us that you don't have to do it perfectly.

If you struggle with your relationship, you have found the right book. If you already have a healthy, functioning relationship, this book will help you maintain your ideal marriage or committed partnership. And if you already have the perfect partner, this book will make you a better person.

Tammy Nelson, PhD

Introduction

The conundrum of romantic love has interested me for as long as I can remember. Having witnessed and experienced firsthand the pain of my own parents' conflicted marriage and divorce, I've always carried within me the heartache of an unhappy partnership. And yet as a girl, I held on for dear life to the glimpses I caught of romantic love. At nine years of age, my best friend and I started a special club dedicated to romantic daydreaming. We constructed scrapbooks of our teenage heartthrobs and buried tinfoil-wrapped time capsules in her backyard, the names of our secret crushes safeguarded within them on scraps of paper torn from our diaries. Even then I sensed the unique potential that lies dormant at the core of intimate bonds.

Sometimes, I actually glimpsed it in the world around me. I remember the first time I noticed my grandfather hug my grandmother when they were picking tomatoes in their garden. She laid her head on his shoulder as he gazed at her and smiled. I saw a neighbor's parents cook together, couples in restaurants reaching out to hold hands. There were people out there who appeared to have developed seen and unseen ways of cross-pollinating everyday interactions with thoughtful gestures and loving acts.

Everyone's early field research on romantic relationships is different. Mine was exciting, heart-wrenching, and messy, like eating pizza in a wind tunnel. The puzzle of romantic love became an urgent personal dilemma. Being successful in love—or at least more successful than my own parents—wasn't as easy as I'd thought it would be. I was convinced that it was a simple matter of combining good intentions with the right partner choice. I married hoping to minimize the mess while finding stability, but four years later, I was signing divorce papers.

In the aftermath of my divorce, the damage my ex-husband and I wreaked on each other seemed to have left us both worse off than if we'd never met and married at all. I had all kinds of questions and no answers. Why did so many romantic relationships start right and end poorly? Why do people choose partners who are unable to provide them with what they need? Why is it that what seems easy to give in the first few months together gets farther away the closer you get to it, like an object in an infinity mirror? Why had the precautions I'd taken to avoid heartbreak and betrayal failed? How could I build a passionate, lasting alliance with a man I loved?

A few years later, after completing a psychology graduate program at NYU and receiving postgraduate training in Imago Relationship Therapy, I began working as a relationship therapist. I saw all kinds of couples. Some struggled with addiction and legal problems. Others had survived the collapse of the Twin Towers and were trying to rebuild their lives and recover from post-traumatic stress disorder. Still others were on the verge of a divorce as they tried to stop an emotional hemorrhage in the wake of an affair. But I also worked with couples who were trying to cope with ordinary, everyday problems: fighting too much, dealing with misunderstandings, trying to forgive each other after a conflict, having trouble listening, failing to take good enough care of themselves, neglecting their own and each other's dreams, struggling with each other's friends and social networks, feeling conflicted about raising children, losing themselves in all-consuming careers, or forgetting to relax and enjoy their lives.

Over the past decade, the work I've done has helped me better comprehend common challenges couples face. It's helped me make some inroads into the conundrum of romantic love and better support couples in their partnerships. I've also learned to approach my second marriage very differently from my first one.

Nearly a decade and a half after my divorce—and three and a half decades after watching my grandparents picking tomatoes in their backyard—I've learned more about what it takes to stop fighting, connect deeply, and live your way into sustainable romantic love. It's less of an end point or a solution and more of a willingness to explore.

Seeing so many couples risk vulnerability and honesty in their communications despite powerful fears of rejection, judgment, and abandonment, I've been consistently awed by the strength of our universally human desire for acceptance and a passionate connection. Adult romantic relationships are one of the best portable laboratories for learning to be curious about the obstacles that get in the way of loving another and being loved back. Embracing these challenges with humility and curiosity, hand in hand with a partner, creates intimacy.

Our romantic choices hold tremendous potential. We can help shape that potential by working together with our mates to set up spaces and places in the midst of our overcrowded, demanding lives to slow down, connect with ourselves, and connect with each other. Partners can take small, doable steps toward their goals.

Couples who face their fears and look at their blind spots—who own their humanity in all its messiness and recommit daily to growth—possess a truly incredible superpower. They can undo destructive communication habits and cocreate the conditions for a lasting love that sustains them and nourishes life around them. You can become one of these couples. You can develop this superpower.

Rainer Maria Rilke's hundred-year-old advice to a young poet is good advice for people learning how to love: "Live the questions now. Perhaps then, someday far in the future, you will gradually, without even noticing it, live your way into the answer." Though it's human nature to want to seek solutions and resolve problems, quick-fix approaches don't work as well with emotional experiences like longing and desire. In fact, they may bypass the growth opportunity available when we just allow ourselves to be present to the uncomfortable process we're in. This may sound like a counterintuitive thing to read in a book that offers 20-minute exercises to help you stop fighting and strengthen your relationship, but in fact, the two go hand in hand. If you're willing to consistently put in the work, you'll be surprised what a difference these small steps can make. This book is all about opening up a space to explore questions and experiences together. Letting yourself be honest and open about the problems you're facing, rather than rushing to find solutions, deepens your capacity to love others and yourselves.

This doesn't mean all relationships or marriages are worth preserving. There are times when holding on doesn't do anyone any good. But if you're in a struggling relationship, ask yourself, "Am I open to learning more about what's *really* going on under the surface between me and my partner?" If the answer is yes, there may be a treasure buried in your frustrations. You may benefit from Rilke's advice to "live the questions now."

HOW TO USE THIS BOOK

If you were about to go on an adventure someplace you'd never been before, you'd probably take some time to think about where you'd be eating and sleeping, what you'd wear, and what to bring to feel safe and secure. You might research the types of electrical plugs that would work where you'd be traveling, consult with your partner about your itinerary and sleeping arrangements, and develop backup plans for when your phone battery dies or if you can't find each other in a crowd. You'd get ready for the adventure and messiness of a new journey, recognizing that it will be stressful at times.

Similarly, a little preparation will set you up to hit the ground running.

I've designed this book to guide you through 52 common relationship challenges, one for every week of the year—from shared decision-making to affairs. These are issues I've found to be common in both opposite-sex and same-sex partnerships and across a variety of age groups, cultural and ethnic experiences, and religious affiliations. I call them challenges, but they're really chances for you to grow.

Each chapter will include the story of a couple working through a challenge, with an analysis of some of the factors involved in their case. I've simplified these cases to offer you a distillation of each challenge that can be approached in a bite-sized chunk. I don't pretend or presume that these case studies are comprehensive. Where possible, I've returned to the same couples throughout the book to illustrate new challenges. Consider these cases starting points for discussion.

I'll introduce you to what are typically milder challenges first, like self-care and listening. Later, when you read about more triggering challenges—intrusive in-laws, for example, or polyamory—you'll have done some work on the foundational challenges. The exercise at the end of each chapter gives you a chance to explore and unpack each challenge as it relates to your partnership through prompts and shared experiences.

To get the most out of this book, I recommend you read through and complete the chapters in the order they're presented. That means going through at least one chapter and one 20-minute exercise with your partner every week. At the end of the year, you can start over, continuing your work and uncovering new layers of the same challenges.

You don't have to go through these chapters sequentially, though. If you're having a specific problem and you want to address it with your partner—"Ruptures," for example—you can jump ahead, read that section, and dive into the exercise. I cross-reference related stories and relevant tools and techniques so each chapter can be approached as a stand-alone exploration. You can work quickly, doing multiple challenges a week, or you can work slowly, reading the chapters first, digesting them, and then coming back to the exercises later.

This book is for couples and individuals interested in a portable, affordable, and sustainable way of working on fighting less and loving each other more. If you're in couples therapy, it can serve as an adjunct to the work you're already doing. My intention is to give you a multiuse tool—a relationship Leatherman, of sorts—compact and versatile, user-friendly, both thought-provoking and task-oriented. Within these pages, I reference the work of coaches, therapists, writers, and thought leaders whose ideas, theories, and research have influenced my own work.

The challenges, check-ins, tips, and prompts presented here are meant to be woven into your life in a way that's organic, meaningful, and right for wherever you are. Well-being in a partnership can sometimes rise and fall like a volatile stock, but if you're consistent in the work you do, you can support meaningful, incremental improvements even with a small-time investment.

Please note that problems related to substance abuse, physical or emotional aggression, or untreated mental illness require a higher level of care than these 52 chapters or any stand-alone book can offer. If you believe abuse or mental illness is impacting you or your relationship, seek professional counseling or mental health services and speak with trusted relatives, friends, or acquaintances about your need for support. A baseline of security and safety is a prerequisite for partners looking to engage in independent couples work.

Each weekly challenge begins with the story of a fictional couple. These stories are drawn from real couples I've worked with in clinical settings, including my private practice, over the last decade. Although I've changed these cases and all potentially identifying information to maintain client confidentiality, I've also done my best to stay true to the underlying dynamics of each case. Couples issues are complex and layered, and there are always many factors at work. In face-to-face therapy, things like mood disorders, unprocessed trauma, and grief can worsen a couple's conflict. A low-level conflict for one couple might be a high-level conflict for another where health issues, attention problems, or a personality disorder are present.

Becoming aware of our own racial, ethnic, cultural, and heterosexual conditioning, and the painful divisions this conditioning can perpetuate, is also a critical necessity in our diverse modern world, and an ethical responsibility for therapists. As objective as I aspire to be, what I present here will be limited by my perspective. You may see yourself reflected in some stories and not at all in others. Although I'm presenting couples from different ethnic, religious, and cultural backgrounds, gay, straight, queer, and transgender, monogamous and polyamorous, this cross section of couplehood is by no means unfiltered or comprehensive.

The exercises that follow each case illustration can be done anywhere. After each suggested exercise, I've provided a sample exchange between a Speaker and a Listener. These samples capture the focus, tone, and emotional deepening that can take place in each exercise. In reality, there are infinite variations on how these exchanges might sound. The most important things to strive for are authenticity and mutual respect.

Before doing the exercises, I suggest you select a physical and/or psychological **Couples Spot**. This is the place where you and your partner will be meeting once a week to explore that week's challenge. You can choose a physical space in your home, a virtual space if you're in different locations, or you can simply shift into an open, curious frame of mind.

You will also be opening a **Couples Time Container**. This is the mutually agreed on and honored length of time, from start to finish, that you and your partner take to complete an exercise. Talk about how you will open your Couples Time Container and decide each week who will begin as the Speaker and who will begin as the Listener. Come up with your own system for dividing your Couples Time Container so that each of you has equal time in both roles.

It's important to negotiate a Couples Time Container with your partner to set the stage for the work you'll be doing. Agree to take at least 20 minutes out of your week, on whichever day works best for the two of you, to meet in your Couples Spot. Program this appointment into your calendars. If you're going to be reading sections of the book together, you may need to factor that into your plan. Opening your Time Container with a particular week's case exploration fresh in your mind can enhance the exercise at the end of the chapter you're working on.

When you're in your Couples Spot and beginning your Couples Time Container, think of it as being "on the job." Your Couples Spot is a consciously created space of emotional safety, and the Time Container is the boundary for how long you have agreed to stay in the Couples Spot. Your role as either Speaker or Listener can help you stay within the bounds of this agreed-upon space.

As the **Speaker**, you're responsible for your thoughts, feelings, and actions. No matter what you're talking about, your goal is accountability: Although you can't always control things that happen in your life, you are the source of how you respond. Take responsibility for your internal experiences and accept your agency and power, even if the only power you have in some situations is to witness and approve of what's going on within you at any given moment.

In the **Listener** role, your job is to allow your opinions, knowledge, and memories to recede into the background. This part of you is rooted in being rather than doing. In the Listener role, you stay present to the Speaker, paying attention to their experience rather than your own reactions—and leaning into points of connection. As soon as you're aware of your own reaction, particularly if it's a "communication stopper" (see page 24), your job as the Listener is to gently notice your reactivity, take a deep breath, and temporarily set it aside so that you can focus on the Speaker once again.

For those who are partnered but choosing to read this book on their own or for people who are single—feel free to follow the guidelines presented for couples with a few adjustments. Be creative! Rather than speaking to a partner, journal your responses to the prompts and then read them out loud, or make an audio recording. Instead of trading roles, reread your entry to yourself, or become your own Listener as you replay the recording you made as the Speaker. For the "eye-gazing" exercise (page 35), look at yourself in the mirror. For Love Catch (page 251), throw your ball into the air as you voice all the things you love about your life.

Have you ever had the experience of talking to your partner and suddenly your stomach clenches? Your partner's face looks constricted or tense, like they're getting defensive. You try to redirect the conversation back to where it was, but it doesn't work. *What on earth just happened?* you may wonder. *We were just talking!*

Talking with our partners can be difficult. The stakes are often higher with vulnerable issues. In this book, I'm inviting you to do something challenging: talk to your partner regularly about things that are hard to talk about. I'm inviting you to approach vulnerable issues head-on, rather than waiting for those issues to blindside you.

Between some sections, I've included Stepping Stones to make talking to your partner a little easier. **Stepping Stones** are meant to inspire and motivate you and your partner to continue on your journey through the exercises and this book. They offer tips, practical advice, and support, often expanding on themes from the case studies.

I'm excited to accompany you on a curated, experiential journey through 52 common couples' challenges. I encourage you to bring yourself wholeheartedly to these pages. Be willing to listen, ask open-ended questions, be gentle and generous of spirit, and assume the best about your partner. Don't give up, even when the work stalls. Meet regularly in your Couples Spot, breathe deeply, embrace the journey, and enjoy the ride.

COUPLES TIME CONTAINER TIPS

Begin your Couples Time Container by setting a timer. If you try to guess the point at which you'll switch roles, it can lead to disagreements and derail your work. Stick to a structure that works for you and keeps you coming back. A reliable and workable structure will help you both remain committed and engaged for the long haul.

When the initial Speaker has reached the end of their half of the Couples Time Container, after the Listener has responded with a closing prompt, switch roles, restart the timer, and repeat the chapter exercise. When the second half of the timer is complete, close your Couples Time Container for now, unless you mutually decide to extend it. Try to wrap up your work with a thoughtful, affirming prompt, like the ones offered at the end of the exercises.

Concluding Couples Time Containers with an expression of physical affection for one another, such as a hug or a kiss or both, brings positive, pleasurable associations to the work you're doing, making it that much easier to return to your Couples Spot in a week's time.

GROUND RULES REVIEW

- Make time to be together: Take at least 20 minutes out of your week to work on your relationship.

- Find and agree on your Couples Spot.

- Negotiate your Couples Time Container.

- Agree on how to initiate the Speaker and Listener roles each week.

- Agree on how to divide your Couples Time Container to ensure each of you speaks and listens equally.

- Use Stepping Stones to support you with process-related tips.

- Reread the section you're working on together, if possible; if you can't, skip to the exercise.

Self-Care

— The Oxygen Mask
(Hanako & Saul)

— Saying No
(Arjun & Susan)

Self-care is at the foundation of a balanced relationship.

1

The Oxygen Mask

Hanako and Saul were stuck in a relationship catch-22.

A petite young woman in her mid-twenties, Hanako was finishing medical school. Her schedule was intense and erratic as she did 12-hour shifts at a local hospital to complete her residency. She was polite and friendly when she spoke, but her eyes looked sad.

Saul, a burly young man with a beard and a crew cut, claimed he was tired. He said that Hanako wasn't supporting him or offering to help when he was overwhelmed. He cooked, kept track of finances, set up date nights, cleaned the apartment, did their shopping, and went out of his way to pick her up from the hospital in the middle of the night.

Listening to Saul's litany of complaints, Hanako looked like a commuter caught in a hurricane without an umbrella.

"How would you feel less taken for granted, Saul?" I asked.

"If she noticed things, like when I need help. If she took care of *me*, sometimes."

"I feel like I offer to help you all the time," Hanako said.

Saul looked confused.

"The other night, I tried to cook. You got irritated," she reminded him.

"Well, with cooking, it's easier if I do it," Saul rationalized.

"And today I went to pick up your shirts—"

"I was already halfway to the dry cleaner," Saul interrupted.

The beauty of being in a couple is that sooner or later, your blind spots emerge. Like many people who struggle with self-care, Saul was doing a good job at taking care of other people: too good of a job, in fact. His self-sacrifice and caretaking were admirable, but they were also obscuring his inability to receive the things he most desired from Hanako: attention, care, and nurturing. Saul had a hard time taking in Hanako's attempts to care for him. This is quite common for over-givers, in fact. Perhaps Hanako could have done more to take care of Saul—she was very busy, after all, but over time she had resigned herself to trying less because she saw she couldn't win. Every time she tried to care for Saul, he dismissed her efforts.

"Saul," I said, "could you do less for Hanako and more for yourself?"

"But isn't that why we're together?" Saul argued, gesturing toward his girlfriend. She looked skeptical. "So that I can take care of her and she can take care of me?"

"That's part of it," I agreed. "But I'm sure you've heard the famous oxygen-mask instructions airline personnel give passengers before takeoff. It's a cardinal rule in relationships. You have to put on your own mask before attempting to help other people."

The oxygen-mask metaphor hit home with Saul, but not because he'd flown in a plane that had lost cabin pressure. He'd suffered from asthma as a kid and learned to administer his own medication when he had trouble breathing. Even as an adult, he still remembered a few situations when waiting for assistance might have had serious or even fatal consequences.

Self-care is often an individual solution to a couples' problem. If we try to get our needs met indirectly, hoping and dreaming that one day our partner will dedicate themselves to caring for us, we're putting a burden on them and a strain on our relationship. Of course, we all want to be with someone who will take care of us, and people in a solid partnership do need to be able to count on each other. That said, if you're not taking care of yourself, in the long run you won't have anything to give another person. In Saul's particular case, his challenges with self-care were the echo of feedback loops and cyclical interactions with important people in his life tracing far back into his history. Because he'd learned to be the "man of the house" as a boy when his mother was sick and his father traveled, his sense of self had crystallized around caretaking. Now, as an adult, his intense, hidden longing for care was pulling him off course. He expected care from Hanako when she was running on empty. The times she did show him care, he rejected it because it wasn't fitting into the model he'd constructed in his head about what caregiving looks like. Shifting this imbalance had to begin with Saul learning to take better care of himself and examining the ideas he had formed around caretaking. Only then could Hanako and Saul begin to discuss the practical aspects of the division of labor in their home and within their relationship.

Exercise

Tell your partner three ways you would like to begin taking better care of yourself in the next week. Notice any fears or assumptions that get in the way of considering these self-care activities.

Be sure to consider activities you typically don't engage in that might bring balance to your life. Someone who socializes a lot and attends a new party every weekend might spend a few hours alone, journaling or meditating. Someone who pours all their excess cash into helping others might buy themselves something they don't "need," or splurge on a pleasurable item or experience, like a book or a foot massage. It's common to feel like you can't afford to spend money on yourself, especially if you're navigating financial stress; at the same time, it doesn't take a lot of money to fulfill a small longing for a cup of tea, a movie, or your favorite food.

Voice the fears or assumptions that have come up. How might you take a step toward doing more genuinely self-caring activities, despite your resistance?

The goal here is to break free of the self-care rut that has you out of alignment with your deeper needs. As the Listener, you can respond to the Speaker's ideas for re-energizing self-care activities with, "I support you in taking genuine care of yourself."

Sample Exchange:

SPEAKER: I want to take better care of myself by reaching out to some of my old friends and trying to organize a get-together somewhere special, like Hawaii, but I'm afraid they'll think it's a silly idea or they'll be too busy, and I worry it's selfish to indulge in vacations with friends. I want to start taking care of myself better by asking you to cook dinner when I'm tired, but I'm afraid you'll feel inconvenienced. I also think it would be taking care of myself if I looked into graduate schools. Feeling like I'm not smart enough and don't deserve to pursue a higher education gets in the way of that one.

LISTENER: Thank you for sharing this with me. Your self-care and my self-care make us stronger because we have the ability to be more generous toward each other when we get what we need from ourselves.

> Your nos are inextricably linked to your yeses.

2

Saying No

When Arjun and Susan started therapy, they were struggling with the seismic shift that had taken place in their lives the moment their baby daughter, Kali, entered it. There were sleep issues, breast-feeding challenges, diaper rashes, and the low-grade anxiety that comes with learning to care for a small, completely dependent human being.

Their biggest problem wasn't new-parenting stress, however. It had to do with trust. Everybody loved Arjun. He was generous and always there for people. Ironically, his likability was part of why Susan didn't trust him.

There were no overt breaches of trust, no patterns of lies in their relationship, but Arjun did have trouble setting boundaries and saying no to family members, colleagues, and friends.

"Sometimes I wonder if you married me to be polite," Susan said. "You're always doing everything you're supposed to do. I don't think I've ever heard you say 'no' to anyone."

Arjun's inability to say "no" had fueled plenty of disagreements between them in the past, but most of the time Arjun found diplomatic ways of placating Susan without having to disappoint others. Now, with the new baby in their lives, the cost of Arjun's compliance was higher. Most recently, he'd said "yes" to his mother's request to spend a week visiting him and Susan (along with Arjun's father). As part of that arrangement, he and Susan would sleep on the futon couch to let his parents have their bed. Susan had reacted to the news with explosive sobbing. The intensity of her reaction had surprised them both.

"Our place is too small," Susan said. "It's barely big enough for the three of us."

Arjun frowned and closed his eyes.

Relationships are lifelines, and we learn early on in our development how to influence the network of connections we're born into. When we explored Arjun's family history, he admitted that saying "no" had never been a real option for him. His parents had come to the United States shortly after he was born and started working several jobs to make ends meet. Arjun's mother had raised him and his two siblings without speaking English, and the stress of assimilating into a new social network had been overwhelming for her. Arjun learned to reduce his parents' stress through compliance. This type of adjustment to a chronic stressor in our childhood is sometimes called a "survival adaptation."

Learning to say "no" to people in his life felt scary to Arjun. Would he lose the love of friends and family?

"'No' tests the health and equity of your closest relationships," clinical psychologist and author Judith Sills writes in her *Psychology Today* article, "The Power of No." "If you feel you cannot say 'no,' at least to some things, some of the time, then you are not being loved—you are being controlled."

Susan softened toward Arjun as she learned more about his mother's struggles, his parents' stress, and the source of his seemingly chronic acquiescence. She had known the facts of his upbringing and his parents' emigration story, but she'd never heard the details in this way, and she began to comprehend why he had developed this pattern of never saying "no."

Arjun began practicing saying "no" in ordinary, everyday situations, such as when someone at work invited him to lunch, or a salesperson in a store asked if he needed assistance. It was hard for him to say "no" unapologetically and without guilt. He motivated himself by turning the practice into a self-awareness game, keeping track of how he felt—one situation at a time and writing down his thoughts, his fears, and his reactive behaviors. He even programmed reminders into his iPhone: *You have a right to say "no." You don't have to keep the peace.*

He and Susan eventually reached an agreement about his family's visit. Arjun booked a room at a nearby hotel. When he shared the change of plans with his mother, explaining that it would be better for them with the new baby and their erratic sleep schedules, his mother was shocked and upset. "You don't respect me," she had said coldly. Although it was hard to experience her disappointment, Arjun held his ground.

Unless a partner is able to say "no" when a "no" is called for, their "yeses" can be hard to trust. As Arjun practiced his "nos" and risked his mother's disapproval, Susan began trusting his "yeses" more, and his genuine commitment to her.

Exercise

The Listener makes a series of simple requests. After each request, the Speaker says either "yes" or "no" as they look the Listener in the eye, noticing what it feels like each time they give their answer. As the Listener, notice what it's like to ask and open yourself to receiving your partner's response. As the Speaker, is it harder to say "yes" or "no"? Which response feels more reflexive or obligatory? What subtle emotions are you aware of with each response?

Sample Exchange:

LISTENER: Can I tell you about my day?

SPEAKER: No.

LISTENER: Thank you. Can I ask you about your day?

SPEAKER: Yes.

LISTENER: Thank you. Can I put my hand on your knee?

SPEAKER: Yes.

LISTENER: Thank you. Can I complain to you about my job?

SPEAKER: No.

LISTENER: Thank you. Can I sing a song?

SPEAKER: No.

LISTENER: Thank you.

SPEAKER: I noticed it's harder for me to say "no" than "yes." Sometimes I said "yes" because I felt anxious that you'd be mad at me if I kept saying "no."

LISTENER: Thank you for practicing your "yeses" and "nos" consciously with me.

stepping stone
SELF-CARE

How do you take care of yourself? Think back to your earliest years and picture yourself as a child. Did you enjoy crafts? Bowling? Sports? Climbing trees? The ways we expressed ourselves freely and creatively as kids can be clues to the self-care we need in order to reconnect with ourselves as adults. Even if you have no intention of climbing trees again, or playing Frisbee, or building sandcastles, ask yourself how you might recapture that sense of wonder, freedom, and play. Can you climb a mountain or a climbing wall? Sketch a flower? Take apart an old watch and look at all the pieces? Skip stones across a river or kick your legs up on a swing? Use these potential self-care activities to begin creating your own list.

- Buy yourself a present without guilt
- Connect with someone you miss
- Dance
- Do yoga
- Eat healthy, flavorful food
- Enjoy tea or coffee
- Exercise
- Get a massage
- Get a medical checkup
- Get enough sleep
- Go out to dinner
- Go to a movie
- Listen to music
- Meditate
- Meet a friend
- People-watch in your favorite café
- Play a board or card game with someone
- Play a musical instrument
- Pursue a dream you've put on the back burner
- Read a book
- Take a mental health day
- Take a walk
- Take 5 minutes to sit quietly
- Take time to journal
- Try something new and adventurous
- Unplug from digital devices
- Write your partner a love letter
- Write yourself a love letter

Communication

— Feeling Your Feelings
  (Lloyd & Janice)

— The Stories We Tell Ourselves
  (Gabriella & Jack)

— Listening
  (Andrew & Jessica)

> Feelings are
> the currency of
> our humanity.

3

Feeling Your Feelings

Many couples with good communication skills struggle with some form of a "feeling problem" that short-circuits their closeness. This was the case with Lloyd and Janice.

When I asked them why they were seeking therapy, Lloyd responded, "Our communication is 95 percent on target. But that last 5 percent is affecting everything else."

As a diplomat, Janice was especially good at being aware of the nuances of people's spoken and unspoken needs and agendas. She exuded authority and self-confidence, though she had an abrupt way of changing the subject in a conversation that could be off-putting and intimidating. Lloyd ran his own life insurance company. His employees liked and respected him. He had a quirky sense of humor and a humble, soulful presence.

Lloyd described one of his major communication frustrations with Janice as the way she spoke to him when she wanted a task completed.

"Can you give an example?" I asked.

"Like when she tells me to put my shoes in the closet instead of in the foyer."

"How else should I say it?" Janice wondered aloud. "That's where shoes go."

"Do you ever tell Lloyd how seeing the shoes in the foyer makes you feel?" I asked.

Janice looked at me askance—as though deciding whether or not to take me seriously.

"How it makes me feel?" she said. "To see his *shoes*?"

"Are you angry when you see them? Anxious?" I persisted.

Janice chuckled, still on the fence about taking me seriously. "I'm not sure I'm anything," she said. "We're talking about shoes here. But you know, maybe I do feel a bit anxious if stuff like that is out of place."

When we followed this thread—Janice's anxiety about household items or shoes being out of place—back through her history, we learned more about her problem with feelings.

Janice believed the best communication happened when feelings weren't involved. As the only child of two older and highly protective Dutch parents, she'd grown up at the center of their world. They'd tried to safeguard her from pain of all kinds, including painful emotions like sadness, inadequacy, and embarrassment. Her parents' overprotectiveness hadn't saved her from these emotional experiences, though it *had* fostered shame about her feelings and led her to believe she had to cope with them on her own.

As she got older, Janice developed mechanisms for avoiding her feelings, called defenses. Psychologically speaking, defenses are strategies we practice, most often unconsciously, to protect ourselves from feared emotional experiences. In accelerated experiential dynamic psychotherapy (AEDP), a feeling and relationship-based therapy model developed by psychologist and author Diana Fosha, clients are encouraged to access the wider array of emotional and relational options available to them that have gone untapped or underutilized. Janice minimized the importance of her emotions. She also kept herself busy with a fierce, tunnel-vision focus on goals and tasks, neutralizing her emotions before they emerged.

"I need to know you're vulnerable," Lloyd said. It had touched him when Janice admitted to her problems with feelings. "It's good when you're not so put together."

"So you like me better when I'm a hot mess," Janice joked.

"Much better," Lloyd said, smiling. "I like you when you're human."

How we deal with our feelings influences how much of our emotional reality we allow ourselves to inhabit. It shapes how comfortable we can get with all of our emotions, from ecstasy to grief, shame to pride, fear to love.

Regena Thomashauer, founder of The School of Womanly Arts and a leading expert in modern feminism, writes in her blog "The 4 Keys to an Extraordinary Life" that life is best when we "play all 88 keys on our piano, not just Middle C, over and over again." For Janice, being an orderly perfectionist in control of every detail in her life was a defense against her own messy vulnerability. She'd been playing Middle C over and over again, limiting the full range of her emotional aliveness.

Exercise

The Speaker names each of the following feelings slowly and consciously, taking a moment to pause and notice how they feel after each word:

- happy
- powerful
- peaceful
- sad
- angry
- scared

What associations arise when you say, "happy," versus when you say, "angry"? Look at the following Feeling Wheel. Are there offshoots of these feelings you hardly ever feel? If so, name them. Are there feelings you feel all the time but keep to yourself? If so, name them.

Sample Exchange:

SPEAKER: When I say the word "happy," I feel sad. There's a sense of loss and exhaustion. I'm always pursuing happiness rather than just feeling whatever I'm feeling, being wherever I am and being okay with that. I have no problem feeling joy, pride, and sadness. I have a hard time feeling anger and helplessness. I'm aware that I cry a lot, so I guess crying is easy for me. My mom always cried, no matter what she felt. I think there's frustration under my tears.

LISTENER: Thank you for giving me this window into your inner world. It's helpful to know more about the different ways you experience your feelings.

FEELING WHEEL

> To rewrite a story,
> you first need to know
> it's a story.

4

The Stories We Tell Ourselves

Gabriella and Jack were in their late thirties. They were both the eldest in their big immigrant families, Italian for Gabriella and Irish for Jack. Each of them was also the first for whom the luxury of a college education had been possible. Gabriella was a tax attorney and Jack was a New York City detective. They'd been living together for a decade, but they both agreed they'd been growing apart for a long time.

"It started a year and a half ago," Jack said. "After your hysterectomy."

When Gabriella first sat down, she had looked as though she was on the verge of tears, but when Jack spoke, she sat bolt upright in her chair. Her eyes narrowed with hostility.

"Because we stopped having sex," she said. "That's why you think it started a year and a half ago. Jesus, I swear, sex really is all you care about, isn't it?"

Jack's face took on a shell-shocked expression.

"Let's back up," I said, sensing we'd just taken the first step into a well-trodden and unhelpful rabbit hole. "Gabriella, I'm going to coach you to say that again, only this time, see if you can take full responsibility for your assumptions."

"It's not an assumption," Gabriella insisted. "I know he watches porn. We don't have sex, so it's like I don't exist for him. He just goes into the basement when he comes home."

"The story I make up is that all you care about is sex," I coached.

"Are you kidding? You want me to repeat that?" Gabriella asked, her face incredulous.

Stories are one of the biggest love-drains in relationships. Prefacing our assumptions with a simple phrase like *the story I make up* can release the death grip of a powerful story. For Gabriella, introducing her judgments of Jack as a *story* about him rather than an objective truth was a way of acknowledging that he was his own person with his own reality.

Gabriella sighed and turned to Jack.

"The story I make up is that all you care about is sex," she said reluctantly.

"And the way that story makes me feel is . . . " I coached, indicating that this was her next line in the script to try out and complete in whatever way felt most authentic to her.

"And the way that story makes me feel is . . . disgusted and angry."

"And when I feel disgusted and angry, I cope by . . . "

A look of comprehension shifted the muscles around Gabriella's mouth and eyes. "If I'm completely honest, I cope by making up *more* stories about how little you care about me, how men can't be trusted. Then I bite your head off when you walk in the door."

Gabriella looked genuinely pleased with herself. It can be a relief when a person sees that they themselves are the birthplace of their relationship horror stories, not their partner. If a potential intruder in a dark room turns into a coatrack when you switch on the light, your sense of safety and ease can be quickly and automatically restored.

Now Jack's eyes were moist.

"Okay, I guess I see why that would not be fun to come home to, and why you might avoid me when you walk in the door," Gabriella said.

Jack shrugged, looking sheepish.

Human beings are storytellers. It's how we make sense of the world. We tell ourselves stories because we're trying to make sense of situations that confuse us, and that's nothing to be ashamed of. Still, it helps to acknowledge that we do this and recognize when our stories become distortions of reality. Figuring out why our partners react the way they do takes patience and humility. We may assume they think or feel like us, or that they act for similar reasons. Making assumptions is often easier than asking our partners what they are actually feeling or thinking. Asking instead of assuming allows us to learn about our partners from the only person who really *knows* them: them!

Seeing, challenging, and interrupting your own horror stories about your mate, as Gabriella did with Jack, can turn intruders into coatracks and reconnect you with what's truly there.

Exercise

The Speaker identifies two of their most familiar stories (see the following "Common Horror Stories" list), then shares situations where these stories frequently pop up in their relationship. What do you feel about yourself, your partner, and your relationship when you believe these stories? How do you cope or react?

COMMON HORROR STORIES

- I'm not good enough.
- I can't get it right.
- I'm broken.
- I'm not lovable.
- I can't trust anyone.
- I'll always be alone.
- I don't fit in.
- I'm too old for love.
- I'm not important to you.
- I'm doomed to failure.
- Everyone abandons me.
- My needs don't matter.
- I'm too much.
- I'll never be fulfilled.
- I'm worthless.
- People always take advantage of me.

Sample Exchange:

SPEAKER: One of my relationship horror stories is that I can't get anything right. I tell myself this story whenever you ask where I put the car keys in a frustrated voice. It makes me feel hopeless and inadequate. I cope by withdrawing and withholding affection, and telling myself other horror stories, such as that we'll never make it as a couple. When I choose to believe these stories, I feel angry and sad. I cope by pouring myself a glass of wine, or spending hours shopping on the Internet.

LISTENER: Thank you for recognizing your relationship horror stories and owning up to them. It frees both of us up to know that they're really just stories, and they don't have to define us as a couple.

True listening
takes practice.

5

Listening

Andrew and Jessica were sitting silently on opposite sides of the
couch in my waiting room. Usually I can hear the faint murmur of
couples chatting through the office wall before I meet them for the
first time, but their arrival seemed to have taken place in a vacuum.

Jessica was of Argentinian descent, though she'd been born in
New Mexico. She was Andrew's second wife. Andrew had come to
the United States from Poland as a young boy. They'd met 30 years
ago when Jessica was one of his engineering graduate students.
Jessica was now in her late fifties and Andrew—still a tenured professor—was eighty. He suffered from rheumatoid arthritis and walked
with a cane. They had two adult daughters, both in college. Their
concern had nothing to do with their age difference or empty nest
issues, however. They had a much more common problem: listening.

"I can't even go into your study," Jessica complained during one
of our sessions, "There's junk everywhere. Your desk is an absolute mess."

"Then don't go into my study," Andrew grumbled. "Problem solved."

"Sure, let the roaches and rats invade us when you leave your half-eaten sandwiches in the garbage can," Jessica said. "Maybe I'll do that one day when I finally pack my bags and leave you, but not just yet."

"Well, you better hurry up and leave me because I may not be around long."

Over the years, Jessica and Andrew had developed two settings when they were together, like an old kitchen appliance: silence or fighting. Their arguments ran the gamut from minor nit-picking to all-out, low-blow character assassination. Their everyday disagreements hovered at around a three or a four on a scale from one to ten, vacillating between petty paper-cut comments to drawn-out, machine-gun defensiveness. When they argued, there was often a level of comfort and familiarity in it, I noticed—a hint of satisfaction on Andrew's face, a pleasurable undercurrent in Jessica's dramatization of her martyrdom. Below the tumult, fights were home.

"Are you willing to listen to each other?" I would ask.

"Sure," Jessica said.

"I'm listening," Andrew said.

And yet as soon as one of them began speaking, the other partner would interrupt, contradict, dismiss, make a face, or launch into a self-righteous tirade.

At our first session, I introduced Jessica and Andrew to the first step of the Imago Dialogue, a communication protocol created by internationally known relationship experts Harville Hendrix, PhD, and Helen LaKelly Hunt, PhD, several decades ago. It's a pivotal tool in Imago Relationship Therapy. The initial step of the dialogue is called "mirroring." It involves setting aside your personal agenda, putting your attention on your partner, and then reflecting back— or mirroring—the words you've heard.

"Why is it important to reflect back what he says when I already know everything about him?" Jessica asked one afternoon. "We've been married for 30 years."

"When you mirror your partner's words and tune in to what they're trying to tell you, you're letting them know you respect them," I said, then added, "even if they're different."

"But she doesn't respect that I'm different," Andrew said, filling his cheeks with air and exhaling emphatically. "She wants me to be exactly like her."

"We'd get along much better," Jessica muttered.

"And be bored out of your minds," I offered in my best impersonal-therapist voice.

They laughed and I joined them.

"True," Andrew said, wiping the moisture from his eyes.

Taking turns speaking conscientiously, and then repeating back each other's words, was a painstaking process for Andrew and Jessica at first. But, gradually, it offset some of their bad communication habits. Rather than focusing on proving each other wrong or contradicting each other, they put their energy into remembering each other's words long enough to be able to repeat or paraphrase them, or checking in to see if they'd heard each other accurately. This was a small step for Jessica and Andrew and a giant leap for their relationship.

After several weeks, I noticed even-keeled conversation and occasional bursts of laughter coming through the walls of the waiting room before our sessions. Andrew and Jessica had begun to develop a new setting other than silence or fighting in their communication repertoire.

Exercise

The Speaker identifies a trait, quality, recent action, or general characteristic about their partner they appreciate, then shares this appreciation in detail. As the Speaker, be sure to pause between ideas and phrases. Wait for the Listener to mirror back what they heard you say, then respond, "You got it," and continue. As the Listener, when you get distracted, simply say, "Can you repeat that?"

If you're the Speaker and your partner misses some part of what you say that's important to you, always try to respond encouragingly, saying, "You got some of it," or, "You got most of it." Then add whatever they missed and wait for them to mirror what you added.

Sample Exchange:

SPEAKER: What I appreciate most about you is that you're sitting here with me right now, doing this exercise, and staying present even though I know you could be at the gym or working on your computer. You're choosing us. That means a lot to me.

LISTENER: I hear you say you appreciate me sitting with you, doing this exercise, and staying present. Is that it?

SPEAKER: Most of it. I know you could be doing other things, but you're choosing us. That means a lot.

LISTENER: Right, you know I could do other things, but I'm choosing us, which means a lot to you.

SPEAKER: That's it. I feel heard.

LISTENER: Thank you for giving me a chance to practice listening with you.

stepping stone
COMMUNICATION STOPPERS

Communication stoppers include subtle or overt judgments, name-calling, shaming, harsh language, finger-pointing, belittling statements, and assuming you know your partner's thoughts, feelings, or motives (see chapter 27).

Covert or silent communication stoppers are often visible or audible to our partner through our posture, tone, and facial expressions, or even just through the "vibe" we give off.

Pay attention to your posture. Relax your shoulders, unclench your jaw, uncross your arms or legs, sit in a position that communicates openness and receptivity. Consciously relax the muscles in your legs, arms, stomach, and groin area. Speak in a warm tone of voice. Remind your partner that if you do happen to show signs of reactivity through your posture, voice, or facial expressions, you'll do your best to breathe through it, recenter yourself, and return to your role as the Speaker or the Listener.

Your Partner's World

— Validation
(Abigail & Yolanda)

— Empathy
(Andrew & Jessica)

Validate your partner
often, especially when
you don't agree.

6

Validation

Abigail and Yolanda had been having a long-distance relationship
for three years, with Yolanda flying to New York to visit Abigail,
or Abigail traveling to Florida to visit Yolanda. When gay marriage
became legal in New York, they only waited three days before getting engaged.

A week later they were in my office.

They'd been getting into repetitive arguments about Greg, Yolanda's
closest friend, whom she'd known since high school. Abigail didn't
want Greg at the wedding. He was vulgar and intrusive. She resented
him for all the times over the past three years that he'd invited Yolanda
to dinners and events while unapologetically excluding her.

Yolanda excused Greg's rude behavior. "Don't take it so personally,"
she told Abigail. She wanted him at the wedding.

Neither Yolanda nor Abigail understood each other's point of
view. As a result, what should have been an eagerly anticipated
celebration of love was looking more like a prelude to a breakup.

"What do you think frustrates Yolanda most about you right now?" I asked Abigail.

"When I don't get the importance of her friendships," Abigail said.

Yolanda nodded, twirling her hair around an index finger.

"Could you try to see the situation through her eyes?" I asked.

"It's hard to see something when you disagree with it," Yolanda said.

Abigail agreed to listen to Yolanda talk about the meaning of her friendship with Greg. She'd feared that listening to Yolanda would be an endorsement of past hurtful behaviors, or an admission that she herself had been wrong to judge Yolanda's friendship with him, but she allowed me to coach her nonetheless, as she practiced mirroring Yolanda's words. This is a form of active listening and the first step of the Imago Dialogue protocol (see page 32). It was easier when she noticed her own reactivity, breathed through it, and stayed focused on Yolanda's words.

The second step of the Imago Dialogue is validation.

"In this step, your goal is to let your partner know you get their logic and their reasoning. Start with the words, 'What you're saying makes sense . . .'"

"I'll try," Abigail said skeptically. "Here goes. What you're saying makes sense. Your friends are like family to you. Greg was there when you were growing up. He attended your college graduation. He knows you. It makes sense you want him to be at our wedding."

Abigail still hadn't agreed with Yolanda. But she had validated her.

"Wow," Yolanda said. "Thank you. That feels really, really good to hear you say."

Our partners want to feel like we "get" them—not just their words, but the *way* they think. As Yolanda felt safer, she was able to share more with Abigail about what it was like to grow up as the daughter of two functional drug addicts, trying to look normal from the outside but always just barely scraping by, afraid of the next crisis. Greg had been her only reliable friend. He'd called an ambulance when Yolanda found her mother barely breathing on the living room floor. He'd gotten her through her mother's hospitalization and grief when her mother eventually died.

Greg had been more than a friend—he'd been her family.

The more Abigail accessed the humility it took to validate Yolanda, the safer Yolanda felt showing her vulnerability. Validation means recognizing that there's more to our partner than meets the eye. Our judgments aren't the same thing as their truths. To validate means to step out from under the shadow of our egos and trust that there's an inherent legitimacy to the way our partners form opinions, generate desires, and reach conclusions. Validation, as the word implies, lets your partner know that no matter how different their reality is from yours, you're able to honor its validity. For Abigail, validating Yolanda helped her taste the freedom and connection that existed when she could relax the death grip of her ego and align with her heart and her relational goals.

Exercise

The Speaker discusses what types of responses make them feel both validated/heard/seen and invalidated/unheard/unseen. The Listener validates the Speaker throughout this process, beginning with the words, *What you're saying makes sense because . . .*

Sample Exchange:

SPEAKER: When a person listens to me without commenting, but just pays attention, it's validating. When you're quietly present and looking at me with warmth in your eyes, like you're doing now, that's also validating. It feels validating if I'm sad and you notice and move closer to me. When people see me struggling and jump in with unsolicited advice, that doesn't feel validating. Mostly, I just want to be heard and to know that what I'm feeling or going through is valid and legitimate.

LISTENER: What you're saying makes sense, because one way to feel someone cares is for them to just be present and attentive. It makes sense you like my attention focused on you because that means I'm with you and not distracted. It also makes sense that when you're sad and I move closer, it feels validating because I'm seeing that you need comfort. It makes sense that just being understood could feel validating, rather than someone jumping in with advice.

> Empathy transcends division and separation.

7

Empathy

It's not unusual for conflicts that occupy a couple's energy and attention to be the outer layer covering deeper issues—protecting them, however unconsciously, from more challenging struggles. As Andrew and Jessica showed each other more respect and care through deeper listening (see chapter 5), the "outer-layer conflict" of the clutter in Andrew's study became increasingly problematic and emotionally charged.

Empathy can't be forced or faked, but it can be practiced. It's the third step, after mirroring and validation, in the Imago Dialogue protocol (see page 32) and the essence of spiritual practices, healing modalities, therapeutic frameworks, not to mention everyday, ordinary moments of connection. Jessica was frustrated with the amount of junk piled on the floors, the desks, and the bookshelves. It bothered her that Andrew collected suitcases full of knickknacks and old letters. Stacks of photo albums blocked the windows. A variety of seemingly useless objects, which Jessica described as "fire hazards," reached to the ceiling and blocked the back door.

"You don't need a broken camera or an ancient bird feeder," she said. "That stuff serves no purpose. It's been rotting away in there for years. It needs to be thrown out."

"The camera was my uncle's," Andrew said. "One of the girls might appreciate it, one day. And the gothic bird feeder is all I have from my parents' garden in Lublin."

"What about the yellow stack of papers on your desk? Boxes of pictures and hotel receipts?" Jessica asked. "Thirty-year-old hotel receipts? Do you need to keep *those*?"

"How does it feel to imagine throwing that stuff out?" I asked Andrew.

"Sickening," Andrew responded. "Paralyzing. My older brother died of pneumonia two years ago. My mother died—how many years was it, Jessie? Before our eldest was born."

"Twenty," Jessica said, her voice low.

"I know it's just stuff, but it's all I have left of my family."

Jessica looked pained as she watched Andrew's face.

"Can you empathize with his difficulty throwing things away?" I asked.

"I imagine it feels painful," Jessica said. "The memories. Sad. Overwhelming."

Andrew nodded. He raised a trembling hand and touched his eyes.

Tears started down his cheeks. "I'm also scared of leaving you alone."

Jessica reached out and took one of Andrew's trembling hands in hers.

"There's so much here," I murmured, feeling the depth of emotion between them.

"I'm afraid, too," Jessica said softly. "Maybe that's why I'm always keeping myself busy. When I imagine you gone and having to go through all of the stuff in your study by myself, seeing all those things, it breaks my heart. I think the grief would overwhelm me."

"I never really considered it from your perspective," Andrew said. "I always just saw you as a neat freak. But when I think about it like that, I can imagine it would feel quite sad and overwhelming. Wondering how you will deal with all of my papers, all the things in there. When I keep postponing cleaning it up or getting rid of it, I imagine you feel ignored."

Jessica nodded. "And hurt," she said. "And unloved."

When couples connect with each other through their hearts—through empathy—the conflict or disagreement between them can be transformed. Empathy enlarges their world. But opening to experiencing empathy, or to receiving a partner's empathy, takes courage. Many of us may strive for empathy in theory, while in reality, being present to the full experience of our partner's emotional truth—without pushing it away, collapsing into it, or trying to fix it—can be disconcerting and intense. And yet it's the heartbeat at the core of connection.

Exercise

The Speaker recalls one time in their life (unrelated to their partner) when they needed empathy. As the Speaker, try to describe in detail how it felt either to receive, or not to receive, empathy.

In the Listener role, empathize with the Speaker's experience by saying, "I imagine you felt . . . " and imagine the Speaker's feelings. Then check in with them to see if any of the feelings you selected resonate.

Sample Exchange:

SPEAKER: When I was around seven, I didn't like "girly" stuff or "girly" games. I didn't even play with girls. One day I was having a Nerf war outside with some neighborhood boys and they started teasing me, saying, "Are you a boy or a girl?" When I told my mom, she said, "You need to act like a girl or kids will tease you." That hurt a lot.

LISTENER: I imagine that when your mom told you to act like a girl or you would get teased, you felt sad, unseen, ashamed, and disappointed. Were those your feelings?

SPEAKER: Yes, they were. I also felt lonely.

LISTENER: You also felt lonely. Did I get it?

SPEAKER: You did. Thank you for empathizing with me.

stepping stone
THE IMAGO DIALOGUE

Relationship experts Harville Hendrix, PhD, and Helen LaKelly Hunt, PhD, created the Imago Dialogue in 1988. It's a foundational tool in Imago Relationship Therapy. Each Imago Dialogue has one topic, agreed on beforehand. It's divided into two parts, giving each person a chance to be in the role of the sender and the receiver. The dialogue starts with the first sender sharing on one topic, using "I" statements and vulnerable language, while the receiver mirrors back what they hear.

Mirroring involves putting your point of view on hold, containing your reactivity, and focusing on what the sender is sharing until they complete their half of the dialogue.

The second step is validation. When you validate your partner, you're letting them know you understand their logic. You're actively approving of the way their mind works, even if you don't agree with them about an issue. You're able to step out of your own view temporarily to see the world from their perspective. Even when you don't agree with your partner, you can still see how and why they think the way they do.

The final step is empathy. In this step, you let your partner know that you are able to imagine their inner reality by making educated, emotionally attuned guesses about what they feel and then checking in with them for confirmation. This step is about connecting with what they're sharing by really taking their experience into your own heart.

Intimacy Issues

— Intimacy Tolerance
(Lloyd & Janice)

— Vulnerability
(Gabriella & Jack)

8

Intimacy Tolerance

Janice and Lloyd, from chapter 3, made major strides in their
communication. Janice paid closer attention to her defenses and
noticed her feelings more often. She risked experiencing a wider
array of emotions with Lloyd, allowing him to catch glimpses of
the raw needs and fears beneath her glossy, high-functioning persona. Seeing her vulnerability allowed Lloyd to respond to her with
patience when she was critical or controlling.

At the same time, although Lloyd appreciated seeing more of
Janice's softness and humanity, his reactions to her vulnerability
often came across as insensitive.

During one of our sessions, when Janice shared about her father's
recent heart attack, Lloyd excused himself and pulled his buzzing
cell phone out of his pocket.

"Sorry," Lloyd said. "I have to take this call."

He had a brief conversation with a refrigerator repairman and
then put his phone away.

"Where were we?" he asked, smiling brightly. When I checked in with Lloyd about his motives for taking a phone call at that moment, just as Janice shared something so vulnerable, he seemed surprised, then remorseful. He hadn't realized he was avoiding the subject of her father and choosing a meaningless call over his wife's important story.

In another session, when Janice admitted to Lloyd how much she valued and depended on him, Lloyd deflected her admission with an insensitive joke.

There are different forces at work in these situations—human responses are layered and complex. Maybe Janice's grief about her father's health situation triggered Lloyd's buried grief for his own dad, who had left his mother when he was a toddler. Maybe he'd been taught that accepting compliments meant you had a big ego. Or maybe his own defenses against feelings kicked in whenever Janice's softer emotions emerged. Lloyd had the capacity for intimacy, but he sometimes felt subsumed by others during intimate moments. He struggled with staying tuned in to his own experience. Sometimes, intimacy didn't feel safe, or it was just uncomfortable to be in the awkwardness of unguarded, earnest connection.

When I suggested we try an "eye-gazing" exercise at the beginning of one of our sessions, Janice was fully on board. Lloyd resisted. He said it reminded him of a kid's staring game. But then he paused, took a breath, and gazed into Janice's eyes for a few seconds.

"There's a feeling of heaviness in my stomach and the muscles in my throat go tight," he told us afterward, describing the experience of discomfort. "It feels like I can't breathe."

Janice, on the other hand, said she could look into Lloyd's eyes indefinitely. She felt a range of mostly exciting and pleasurable emotions when she gazed at him.

As Lloyd connected to the sensations this exercise evoked, old experiences and memories resurfaced. His mother had always treated him as an emotional confidant. He had listened to her complaints and even held her when she cried. Lloyd remembered feelings of guilt, anger, and confusion when his mother hugged him or when she shared information he didn't want to know. As an adult, too much intimacy signaled danger and loss of self.

Understanding why he behaved insensitively toward Janice in emotionally intimate moments gave a context to their different fears and needs around intimacy. It also motivated them to stretch out of their intimacy comfort zones. For Janice, this meant checking in with Lloyd to assess his comfort level during intimate moments. For Lloyd, reminding himself he had a choice with Janice in a way he'd never really had with his mother, gave him more courage to connect.

Working together as a couple requires a joint sensitivity to how intimacy feels to each of you. Do you like it or do you get uncomfortable in intimate situations? Being curious about your partner's comfort level with emotional closeness is a step toward reducing the push-pull of your dynamic in this area. Self-awareness, direct communication, and compassion for one another's desires and fears can lead to a more secure experience of intimacy. Begin tuning in to the ways you may be unconsciously avoiding intimacy, as Lloyd did with Janice when he took the call during our session. Do you break eye contact prematurely, change the subject, pick at your nails, grow restless, or feel an urge to open the refrigerator or check your phone? Keep a list of interpersonal quirks and behavior patterns you engage in regularly, or ask your partner to tell you what they see. If you can take in your partner's feedback, it may help you soften into what's beneath your defenses.

Exercise

Stare into each other's eyes for two minutes without turning away. It's okay to giggle, cough, mutter, mumble, grow restless or shift your body around, as long as you do your best to bring your attention back to each other's eyes and to taking in the moments of stillness between you.

The Speaker then talks about what they saw, experienced, and felt. This activity can be surprisingly intense and scary, so it's okay to acknowledge that. What felt scary? What felt awkward? Did you feel anything that surprised you? What did you notice about your partner that seemed new or different?

At the end of the Speaker's time, the Listener thanks them.

Sample Exchange:

SPEAKER: When I looked into your eyes, I felt a jolt of energy in my body. I felt nervous. I thought, "This is your wife here, don't be nervous." Then I noticed tension in my chest, almost a clamp. I wanted to get up. That's when I had a bit of a coughing fit. When I paid attention to your smile and the fact that your eyes are flecked with yellow and green, I relaxed, and I felt this wave of gratitude. It feels good to *really* look at you and see you.

LISTENER: Thank you for having the courage to be intimate with me and for giving me a chance to practice being intimate with you.

Vulnerability is the
gateway to intimacy.

9

Vulnerability

As with most couples, Gabriella and Jack, from chapter 4, faced multiple, interconnected areas of challenge in their pursuit of deeper connection. As Gabriella made headway in identifying her stories and containing her negative feelings toward Jack, something unexpected happened. Jack began to get irritable. He pushed her away.

"I'm just not in the right headspace to connect when I get home," Jack said.

"When I try to cuddle up next to you on the couch after dinner, you tell me you're not in the mood for affection. Or you snap at me," Gabriella said. "It seems like you're mad at me."

Although Jack hadn't been escaping to the basement as much as when they first came to therapy, he had started to find new ways of emotionally distancing himself from Gabriella. The more patient she was with him, the more irritable he became.

"What do you think you're looking to get from therapy?" I asked one day.

"I don't know," Jack responded. "I'm just trying my best."

"And what does that feel like," I asked, "being here and trying your best?"

"I'm not sure," Jack said. "It doesn't feel like anything."

"Scary? Neutral?" I persisted. "Numb?"

"Probably 'numb' would be the best description."

"Could you tell Gabriella about the numb feeling?"

When Gabriella leaned an inch or two closer to his chair, I noticed that Jack subtly, almost imperceptibly, leaned back, as though the distance he needed to maintain between himself and Gabriella was as much physical as it was emotional.

"I don't like being here," he said. "That's the truth. So I go numb."

"And if you didn't go numb?" I asked. "What would it feel like to be here?"

"Bad," he said. "Like having no skin."

"That sounds painful," I said.

"It is," Jack said. "It's not something I like. But I come for Gabby."

"Is there anything we could do here that would make it feel safer?" I asked.

"You could get me a new job," he said. Jack was a detective.

"Tell Gabby what it's like to do your job and come home to her. Or what it feels like to come here to therapy." I was getting a hunch about what might be working against their intimacy.

"You really can't know what it's like," he said. "I see things in people's homes, the kids, and what goes on in places where people aren't getting the help they need. Showing up at a crime scene after a shooting . . . it's hard." Jack stared at the floor.

"Can you look at Gabriella?" I suggested gently. Her eyes were brimming with tears as she listened. Jack glanced up, then looked quickly away again.

"What's it like to see Gabriella's face?" I asked.

"It's hard. Because then I have to go back to my job and feel numb again so I don't feel bad. I can't go to work and feel things. It would hurt too much."

This was the beginning of our exploration into Jack's invulnerability. He was caught between two different worlds with widely divergent norms and expectations: the world of law enforcement and the world of intimate relationships. Even for many couples who don't straddle these extremes in their career and home life, vulnerability can be scary. Many of our most painful experiences take place when we're undefended, and we receive powerful negative messages both in our families and in our culture equating openness with weakness and weakness with danger. And yet invulnerability makes intimacy impossible.

In her book *Daring Greatly*, vulnerability researcher and University of Houston professor Brené Brown says, "Our sense of belonging can never be greater than our level of self-acceptance." For Jack, learning to be vulnerable meant acknowledging the tragedy he witnessed every day at his job, the pain it triggered in him, and the ways he felt compelled to bury that pain as a form of self-protection. In fact, Jack needed to call on a degree of invulnerability at work to be able to function and be of service in his job. The problem arose when he rejected his vulnerability and couldn't make the transition out of his work persona. He and Gabriella agreed on a rule that helped them both: for 30 minutes after Jack came home, Gabriella would pretend Jack wasn't there. She wouldn't speak to him or ask him questions; she would simply let him decompress. When he was ready, he signaled his intention to connect with the words, "I'm home." Supported by Gabriella's compassion, Jack took steps toward balancing his worlds.

Exercise

The Speaker tells the Listener about one difficult vulnerable moment they've experienced. What fearful messages did you come to associate with vulnerability from this experience? What's one positive and expansive moment of vulnerability you've experienced? What positive messages about vulnerability did you internalize? Which defenses do you use to be invulnerable? Make a commitment to tell your partner when you're feeling vulnerable.

Sample Exchange:

SPEAKER: One of the most difficult moments of vulnerability I experienced was when I was on stage in third grade and I forgot my lines. I remember the silence in the auditorium. What I came to believe then about vulnerability was that you can't put yourself out there and risk being seen because you'll make a fool of yourself. I had a positive experience being vulnerable when I admitted to a friend that I was envious of her. She hugged me and thanked me for my honesty. The message I internalized then was that vulnerability clears the air and brings you closer to people. I commit to telling you when I'm feeling vulnerable rather than ignoring my feelings, judging you, starting a fight, or giving up on us.

LISTENER: Thank you for your willingness to question your negative messages about vulnerability, and for your vulnerability in our relationship.

stepping stone
INTIMACY COMFORT LEVELS

Where do you think you fall on the Intimacy Spectrum?

The Intimacy Spectrum

WARY ⟨————————————————————⟩ HUNGRY

    1   2   3   4   5   6   7   8   9   10

As a couple, you will probably have different tolerance levels for intimacy. Also, your tolerance levels will fluctuate depending on situations and the amount of stress in your lives.

For a partner who is easily overwhelmed by closeness, 20 minutes in a Couples Spot can feel like a long time. For this type of partner, connection may feel risky. An intimacy-wary partner will expand their capacity for closeness a little at a time. When their intimacy-wary predisposition is respected and taken into consideration, expansion can be smoother. Intimacy-wary partners can feel flooded when they're pressured into closeness.

For a partner who hungers for intimacy, 20 minutes can feel like twenty seconds. Intimacy-hungry partners want more closeness. Often, they can't understand why closeness doesn't feed and sustain their partner in the same way it feeds and sustains them.

Being sensitive to the differences between you and your partner, particularly within your Couples Time Container, can increase your connection as you complete these exercises together.

Taking Responsibility

— You Should Know What I Need
  (Gerald & Luke)

— Psychological Ownership
  (Abigail & Yolanda)

— Projection
  (Hanako & Saul)

"Shoulds" are one way
we avoid taking responsibility
for our needs.

10
You Should Know What I Need

Gerald and Luke had met on a cruise and had been dating for six months. Gerald was a rich, charming, high-powered business consultant with a George Clooney smile, formerly a Wall Street broker, and Luke was a James Beard Award finalist. He dreamed of becoming a celebrity chef. With his well-nourished belly, tattoo sleeves, and inch-wide earspools, he looked the part. Although Gerald was two decades older than Luke, he had a boyish, playful energy about him.

Gerald shrugged when I asked them about their goals for therapy. "It was his idea."

"I don't think he knows how to love," Luke said.

"Translation: I'm not a mind reader," Gerald corrected him.

"Is there a recent situation that upset you?" I asked Luke.

"He never stops by my work." Luke's face reddened. "He never surprises me, visits, or shows any interest in my job. They had a party in my honor last week and he didn't show up. People at work think I'm single."

"You never officially asked me to come to that event," Gerald said. "How am I supposed to know it's important and I'm expected to come if you don't make it clear to me how much you want me there?"

"You *should* know it's important," Luke said. "But I don't *expect* you to know."

"Getting your needs met is going to involve doing three things," I told Luke. "First, taking responsibility for your needs; second, expressing them; and third, receiving Gerald's *attempts* to meet them as forms of love in and of themselves, even if his attempts miss the mark."

"Don't look so excited," Gerald said when Luke continued to stare at me.

Too many "shoulds" in a relationship may indicate boundary problems. Boundaries are the invisible lines—or zones—that separate our own internal world from the world outside of us, including our partners.

In her book *Facing Codependence*, educator and best-selling author Pia Mellody describes two kinds of boundaries, internal and external, and subdivides each of these boundaries into serving three functions: 1) to prevent others from invading our space, 2) to prevent us from invading others' space, and 3) to allow us to be who we are in our own right, distinct from people around us.

When Luke blamed Gerald for not intuiting and fulfilling his needs, and then subtly and repeatedly pressured or punished him with "shoulds," Luke's internal boundaries were failing him.

"Setting Gerald up for success means that you describe your needs clearly," I encouraged Luke. "Describe the situation, your feelings, and what you need from him."

"The situation always changes, but in this case, it's at my restaurant. Honestly, I feel proud and important at work. I'm really a big deal now, but when you never come by and see me in that space, in my element, I feel hurt and ignored," Luke said.

"Now take a moment and feel your need. Describe it if you can," I said.

"I need to know I'm on your mind when I'm not with you. I never felt that growing up, in and out of foster care. Nobody showed up to my school events and graduations."

"Oh, baby," Gerald said with uncharacteristic warmth.

Luke wasn't used to taking responsibility for what he needed and asking for it. Giving up his "shoulds" was a process that required ongoing boundary work. We began by looking at ways Luke could appreciate the steps Gerald was already taking to try to give him what he asked for, even though he "had to" ask for things, and even though Gerald's attempts were imperfect.

Whether or not you buy into the theory that all humans long to reexperience life in the womb, everyone has felt a desire for easy, effortless, reliable comfort. At the same time, making sure we get our important needs consistently met as adults is no one's job but our own. It's also never guaranteed, even when we do the challenging work of recognizing and asking for what we want directly and respectfully. And yet asking in this way does improve our chances.

Satisfying our needs is a gift our partners give us. Being responsible calls for a willingness to ask clearly and vulnerably for what we want, and to tolerate disappointment.

Exercise

The Speaker shares one of their "shoulds," or assumptions, about "the right way to behave." For example, "You should take care of me when I'm sick."

Remake this "should" into a clear and responsible request. Here's a formula for transforming "shoulds" into responsible requests.

"When I'm _____ [your vulnerable situation],

I feel _____ [feelings], and I defend myself

from these feelings by _____ [defensive reaction].

I fear _____ [interpersonal fear].

What I need is _____ [interpersonal need or desire].

It would help me if you would _____

[one specific, doable action]."

Sample Exchange:

SPEAKER: When I'm lying in bed sick, I feel helpless and weak, and I act angry and irritable. I'm afraid you won't love me as much when I'm not strong. What I really need is for you to bring me orange juice, take my hand and sit beside me for a minute, and say, "I'm here for you, sweetheart, I hope you feel better."

LISTENER: Thank you for taking responsibility for your needs.

What you don't own psychologically, owns you.

11

Psychological Ownership

Abigail and Yolanda, from chapter 6, went to Costa Rica for their honeymoon. Two weeks after they returned, they were eager to show me a picture of their wedding ceremony and talk about adventures they'd had on zip lines, jungle hikes, and volcano tours.

At the same time, there was trouble in paradise. Yolanda's moving pod had arrived and they'd been transfering her stuff into Abigail's industrial loft in Jersey City. There were pieces of furniture that didn't work in the new space and would have to be sold or donated to Goodwill.

"It seems like you've been angry," Yolanda said. "At night, you've been turning your back when I get in bed. That wasn't how you acted in Costa Rica."

"I'm exhausted," Abigail said defensively. "I've been helping you move and I've also been catching up at work. I'm not a freelancer; I can't sleep late and hang out all day."

"Is that a jab?" Yolanda asked. She worked as a freelance web designer.

"It's a fact," Abigail said.

Yolanda pursed her lips and looked away.

Psychological ownership is different from the ownership of property or possessions. To own something psychologically means to admit to a quality, trait, action, feeling, or behavior that may be hard for you—or others—to see or acknowledge, such as judgment or ignorance. Although sometimes positive qualities or feelings such as confidence or joy can also feel dangerous to "own," in the long run, whether what we feel is viewed as "positive" or "negative," psychological ownership of the full range of our experience strengthens us.

"You've been living in your place alone for years, Abigail," I reflected. "Yolanda has visited, but this move is much more permanent. It would be normal to have some feelings about what's happening, to feel unsettled, and to be struggling."

"I'm not struggling!" Abigail blurted out. "I'm afraid."

She grabbed a tissue and covered her face and eyes.

Yolanda uncrossed her arms, relaxed her jaw and leaned forward.

"I'm afraid of trusting," Abigail said, her voice quieter. "Trusting that we're family now. It's something I've wanted my whole life, more than anything. Now that it's happening, part of me thinks it's a trick, or that it'll go away. What if it doesn't last? I'm afraid I wouldn't recover."

Yolanda's eyes widened.

"Can you mirror back what you heard her say?" I asked.

"You're afraid," Yolanda murmured softly. "You've always wanted a family but now that I'm moving in, you don't trust that you can count on me. You think it can't last."

Abigail nodded.

"That's right," she said.

Abigail was taking psychological ownership of her emotions. She was disentangling her past from her present and recognizing that she was the one creating her current reality—not Yolanda. By acknowledging her fear and resisting the temptation to shirk ownership, she was also implicity establishing boundaries. No matter how close they were, she was separate from Yolanda. She couldn't control or manage Yolanda's reaction to what she revealed and yet she was sharing, anyway. Whether Yolanda stayed neutral, got angry, questioned her commitment, or pulled away—all of that wasn't within Abigail's realm of control. Ownership is an act of faith.

Far too often, we hold our psychological cards close to our chest in relationships in an attempt to protect ourselves, micromanage our partners, or cope with our own self-judgment. Speaking and acting without taking psychological ownership for our inner reality confuses our partners, but when we risk showing our partner our cards—as Abigail did by sharing her reactions to Yolanda moving in and becoming her "family"—we level the playing field and create the possibility for collaboration. It no longer becomes about trying to come out on top. Instead, you're allowing your partner to know vulnerabilities that could put you at a disadvantage, but at the same time, if they're received with compassion, build trust and draw your partner closer. Psychological ownership is a way of standing in the truth of who you are even when it feels risky.

Exercise

The Speaker takes psychological ownership of one thing they do that they find it hard to admit to. Do you withhold praise, or offer luke-warm reactions to things your partner is proud of or excited about? When your partner makes an effort to please you, do you grunt your acknowledgment or ignore what they've done altogether? Do you criticize your partner when they're cheerful or in a good mood because you feel left out or threatened? Do you pick on people your partner admires because you get jealous and insecure, at times?

Sample Exchange:

SPEAKER: I own that I have poor boundaries in my friendships. Sometimes I feel a sense of petty satisfaction when you're upset. It's like I'm getting back at you for not giving me more of the closeness I want and expect. I know it irritates you when I hang out with my single friends, or go sailing, or take a weekend trip. I guess I can try to own my hurt and sadness at wanting more connection from you, even though it feels embarrassing, and then handle these feelings in a less passive-aggressive way.

LISTENER: Thank you for having the courage to take psychological ownership. I see your humanity, and I appreciate how you're recognizing and voicing your needs.

What we can't
tolerate in ourselves,
we reject in others.

12
Projection

Projection, unrecognized, sabotages relationships.

Hanako and Saul, from chapter 1, had a lot going for them as a couple. Saul worked on his self-care and began expecting more realistic care from Hanako. He became more receptive to the care she did offer him. As Saul grew less critical and more receptive, however, Hanako seemed to become increasingly dissatisfied. Her stress level was high as she completed her medical residency, and he tried to be patient, but it wasn't easy. Her dissatisfaction seemed directed specifically at him.

"I don't know if this can work," Hanako said vaguely during one of our sessions, gazing at the floor. "I really just think our personalities are too different."

"It hurts when you say that," Saul said. "It's like you're saying I'm not good enough for you and you're about to break up with me."

Saul spoke calmly, but Hanako flinched as though he'd yelled.

"That's what I mean," Hanako said. "You're too angry."

"I'm actually not angry. Right now, I feel sad," Saul said. "It hurts to think you'd let what we have go because you've made some kind of mysterious private decision about who you think I am."

"Can you tell Saul what's hard for you to deal with about him?" I asked Hanako.

"Your anger, mostly," Hanako said, in her polite, even-keeled voice. "I don't like it. It bothers me when you get angry at people. Like when our landlord wouldn't fix the shower. Or your brother last week. Your anger and your irresponsibility, too. Like going to Peru to do an Ayahuasca retreat. I don't think that works in a long-term relationship."

"Some of the qualities you see in me are anger, irresponsibility, and recklessness," Saul said, breathing deeply. He'd been practicing mirroring (see chapter 5) with Hanako and knew from previous sessions that it's a good thing to do when you feel triggered, or even just when you're at a loss in a difficult conversation with your partner.

"I can't accept those things," Hanako said.

"Would it be okay to go a little deeper into what these qualities say about you?" I asked Hanako. "Maybe we can look at why they feel so risky and unacceptable."

Hanako indicated her willingness with a nod. We'd done similar exercises in the past and, for the most part, she knew what to expect. I guided her to close her eyes and connect with her body. She sank back slightly in her chair.

"See if you can sense any anger in your body right now. Notice if there's a place where it exists inside of you, not just outside in Saul."

Hanako shook her head.

"No anger," she said. "It's fear."

"When you stay with the fear, what do you notice?"

"Memories. My father yelling at my mother. I'm scared he'll hurt her. She's very irresponsible. That's what makes me angry," Hanako said, opening her eyes suddenly. "My mother didn't think about the consequences of her lovers. It affected us all."

By identifying where the qualities she judged so harshly in Saul originated in her own life, it was easier for Hanako to connect the dots. She began taking responsibility for her projections.

Over time, she recognized she felt angry a lot: about her parents, her childhood, the stresses of medical school, daily indignities in an overcrowded city, the sexism and prejudice she experienced as a Japanese woman in a white-male-dominated profession. She could be irresponsible and reckless herself and had jeopardized her own physical safety in medical school by drinking too much. There were ways that even now, despite being studious and ambitious, she had accumulated debt on credit cards and failed to prioritize her own health.

Hanako recognized she could erode her bond with Saul by judging him for the very qualities she was unable to tolerate in herself. When Saul displayed tendencies or traits she didn't want to connect with in her own personality or character, it made her feel anxious and out of control. By recognizing this and voicing it, they were both able to better understand the emotional undercurrents of the situation and empathize with one another's position.

Exercise

The Speaker identifies three of the top negative characteristics they see in other people, aspects that frequently bother or irritate them. As the Speaker, tell your partner how these three negative features also exist within you.

Sample Exchange:

SPEAKER: The three things I see in other people that really bug me are sloppiness, irresponsibility, and pessimism. I am sloppy, too, sometimes. My purse is a mess, and so is my car. There was nowhere I could let things slide growing up, so I've created these little pockets of chaos. I know I can be irresponsible. Like the time I missed my flight because I was shopping in the airport mall. I'm secretly pessimistic, I guess, though I hate admitting it. I'm afraid I'll become like my mother and be a worse pessimist than she was.

LISTENER: Thank you for being willing to take responsibility for your projections. This frees me up to be a bit more honest, and to be more understanding of your annoyance with me for things I do.

stepping stone
VENT BOXES

A Vent Box is a tool you can use to express frustrations. Keep them short. If you've ever seen a two-year-old pounding on the floor and yelling, you understand why freely expressed frustration can be hard to tolerate. At the same time, intimate relationships offer us an opportunity to acknowledge and release pent-up frustrations in the presence of someone who cares about us and knows us well enough not to judge us based solely on this particular display of emotion.

If your partner agrees to give you a Vent Box, give yourself permission to have an "adult tantrum." Forget about being spiritual, rational, thoughtful, kind, or good. Express your anger, jealousy, resentment, and bitterness.

Experiment with ways to do this that feel authentic without being triggering to your partner. People tend to feel safer witnessing strong emotions when they're under control and know that it will come to a predictable end. Maybe you allow yourself to raise your voice, make faces, use "bad words," or punch the air.

When your time is up, end the Vent Box on a positive note. Feel free to laugh about what just happened. Did it feel good to throw a tantrum? Shift back to your adult self by sharing something about your life that you're proud of or grateful for. Move on by transitioning to a pleasurable activity, such as listening to music, going for a run, or cooking a meal.

Example: Jake enters the kitchen where Sam is on the computer.

Jake: Hi, I'm so glad I'm home! I'd love a minute-long Vent Box on Rachel.

Sam: Sure, I can do that. Let me get off the computer. Okay, go ahead.

Jake: (Raising his voice) I'm so sick of Rachel's passive-aggressive comments! I hate her! She drives me crazy! Why can't she get out of my face? Arghhhh! She's the most patronizing, irritating, controlling person I've ever met. I wish she'd move to Australia!

Sam: Thanks for allowing me to witness you. How would you like to close your Vent Box?

Jake: Thanks for witnessing. Let's go for a short walk.

Love Rituals

— Check-Ins
  (Randy & Felice)

— Takeoffs and Reentries
  (Elena & Donald)

— Appreciations and Gratitude
  (Candace & Sean)

13

Check-Ins

Attractive, charming, and funny, Felice and Randy were the envy of many of their friends. They had a beautiful house overlooking the Potomac River in the middle of Georgetown in Washington, DC. Their smart, healthy, 10-year-old twin girls went to a prestigious private school that a former president's children had also attended. Randy had a high-powered government position, and Felice enjoyed many of the freedoms of a stay-at-home mom with elementary-school-aged kids. She also did volunteer work and led meditation retreats twice a year at a local retreat center.

But, as a couple, they felt disconnected.

"Maybe this is revisionist history," Felice said, "but I'm beginning to doubt we were *ever* connected. I know we look good from the outside . . . but maybe it's always been a show."

Randy stared regretfully at her.

"You're looking at me like I'm crazy," Felice said, tossing her hair back, away from her face.

"Have we been disconnected for a while?" Randy asked. "Yes. Do we need to change? Yes. Have I been guilty of avoiding the problem? Yes."

"That's an understatement," Felice said.

"Okay, I've been very guilty of avoiding the problem," Randy continued, "but that doesn't mean we've never genuinely loved each other or don't love each other now."

Randy and Felice had an excess of what so many people strive for: status, physical attractiveness, leisure time, youth, material wealth, intelligence, and a healthy, thriving family. It was as if they lived at the center of an extravagant, all-you-can eat buffet that was perpetually stocked with delectable foods. But one essential ingredient was missing: genuine connection. The absence of connection made all their delicacies and delights less appetizing. A lack of genuine connection had been leeching essential nutrients from their relationship.

"Do you check in with one another over the course of your day?" I asked.

"Not really," Randy said pensively. "No, I guess we don't."

"We do things together, like attend the girls' lacrosse games," Felice said. "We sit side by side a lot, at functions and formal dinners, or in the car, or at the gym watching our girls at sporting events. But it feels like there's a gulf between us. I don't know what he's thinking, and he doesn't seem to care what I'm thinking or feeling. It's sad."

There were years of unexplored misunderstandings and buried hurts between them, and our work took time. It was like dismantling a house, creating a new foundation, and rebuilding the house with a new design from the ground up. At the same time, Felice and Randy continued in the old structure. Psychologically speaking, they were living in a construction site.

We looked more closely at Randy and Felice's communication and intimacy challenges. We also focused on identifying old relationship horror stories (see chapter 4). Randy and Felice practiced taking psychological ownership, recognizing their projections, and speaking from the heart. And more often than they wanted to, they slipped into old patterns of reactivity and blame, felt hopeless, and were tempted to give up.

Love Rituals are new habits couples develop to generate a loving connection on the spot. They function as makeshift emotional tents you can pitch anywhere anytime to create a sense of safety and togetherness. For Randy and Felice, they were a lifeline to connection.

Check-ins, as the title of this chapter suggests, were the Love Ritual they used most often. Check-ins inject authenticity and presence into your interactions and, best of all, they're quick: no more than a minute or two per person. They're also judgment-free. This makes them easy to access and give, once you trust you're safe to share, even if you and your partner are very busy.

Randy and Felice opted for an intensive check-in program for one week to jump-start their connection. They did their first check-in of the day when they woke up. They called this the "dream check," where they told each other briefly what they remembered about their dreams. They did a "day check" before Randy left for work, sharing their hopes for the day and one or two anxieties. They connected once during the day via FaceTime with a "feeling check," sharing raw feelings honestly, followed by a one-sentence elaboration on the trigger of the feeling. Before bed, they did a "night check" focusing on what they wanted to let go of before bed. By the end of the week, they felt closer. Taking in more of their partner's inner world regularly, in small doses, reminded them of what they loved and valued about each other, above and beyond the roles they assumed and the daily routines they fulfilled. By the second week, they found that even just doing one check-in daily helped them maintain a degree of nourishing connection.

Check-ins are brief glimpses into your partner's heart, behind the social masks. They're a way of weaving your daily experiences into those of your partner. Through Check-ins, Randy and Felice developed a taste for authenticity.

Exercise

The Speaker does a Feeling Check-in and either a Day or a Night Check-in. Remember, Check-ins are full-body experiences. Take a moment to be aware of your sensations in the moment. Does your stomach feel tight? Is there a heaviness in your chest? Get present to whatever your body is telling you. Then connect with your feelings, your hopes for the day, or with the things you want to let go of from the day that's already passed. Use Check-ins as an opportunity to drop the multiple façades you may need to wear to function efficiently in the world. As the Listener, feel the gift of presence as the Speaker shares. As the Speaker, take in the Listener's attention and curiosity.

Sample Exchange:

SPEAKER: For my Feeling Check-in, I sense I'm anxious, happy, and sad. I'm anxious about all the good stuff that's happening in our life and I'm afraid of the other shoe dropping. I'm happy because we're connecting. I'm sad because my hamstring pain and arthritis remind me of my mortality and I'd rather not think about that. For my Night Check-in, what I want to let go of is my boss's criticism.

LISTENER: Thank you for being willing to check in with me like this. I look forward to practicing Love Rituals more regularly as a way of making connection a habit that nourishes us.

> Partnership is your mother ship: notice the takeoffs and reentries.

14

Takeoffs and Reentries

Elena and Donald saw themselves as a happy couple. They got along well, loved spending time together, and always looked forward to reconnecting after periods of separation, whether they'd been apart for a few hours or a few days.

But when Elena accepted a senior position in her firm that required monthly travel, a painful pattern developed. I've seen different versions of this pattern in many relationships. There's a transition that occurs as partners move out of the world they share together into separate individual worlds, or as they come back into their shared couple's world. The shift can seem unremarkable on the surface, but without awareness or handled haphazardly, these transitions are potential minefields. Stan Tatkin, developer of PACT—a Psychobiological Approach to Couple Therapy—calls these junctures

"Launchings and Landings" in his book *Wired for Love: How Understanding Your Partner's Brain and Attachment Style Can Help You Defuse Conflict and Build a Secure Relationship*. He encourages couples to create more safety at the transition points of bedtime and waking, as well as at the moments during the day when they separate and reunite. Borrowing from Tatkin, I call these junctures "Takeoffs and Reentries."

Elena and Donald had no problem with their Takeoffs. Whenever she traveled, he would drive her to the airport himself. They kissed like teenagers, agreed to call each other regularly, and said goodbye. Their problems surfaced at Reentries. Typically, despite their best intentions, their greetings went awry as soon as Elena came home. She always seemed to show up on the doorstep with her suitcase at the exact moment when Donald was in the middle of an important task. As a result, he was unable to give her a warm greeting. Or else Elena was preoccupied or distracted. One of them would invariably say or do the wrong thing—or fail to say or do something "right." A comment that might have been innocuous at a different point in time landed like a spark on an oil spill during their Reentries. Feelings got hurt, mean things got said, and both Elena and Donald ended up retreating to their respective corners of the house when what they longed for was a happy reunion.

"What do you expect when Elena comes home?" I asked.

"These days?" Donald said. "I'm expecting her to be stressed."

"I know you are," Elena said, "It becomes a self-fulfilling prophecy."

"You walk right past me with your suitcase. How did I make that happen?"

"I walk past you because I know you feel pressured to perform a 'happy greeting,'" Elena said. "You've told me you feel like I expect you to drop everything and recite your happy lines. I'm only walking past you because I'm trying to give you the freedom and time to come to me whenever you're ready to connect."

"But that only makes me feel like I keep failing you as a partner," Donald said.

"What could she do when she comes home that would feel better?" I asked.

"I guess if you said, 'It's good to be home and, wow, thanks for the flowers,'" Donald said. "And, 'Is that the smell of a delicious home-cooked meal?' I'd feel better if you'd just notice something I've done to prepare for your return."

"Sure, I can try to do that," Elena said, laughing.

"What could he do to help you feel welcomed and more relaxed?" I asked.

"If you gave me a heads-up on what you've done so I don't over-look it," she decided. "Send me a text saying, 'I've bought flowers, cleaned up, and made dinner.'"

"Skip the element of surprise?" Donald asked.

"Yes, definitely skip that," Elena said. "I'd rather just know. When you act nervous or distracted, I read that as you wishing I'd stayed away longer. Then I get stressed and irritable."

"And when you're stressed," Donald said, "I go to 'I'm a failure.'"

We identified choice points where both Elena and Donald had options. They started to challenge some of their relationship horror stories (see chapter 4) and recognize projections. They were also able to ask for what they needed. With practice and experimentation, troublesome Reentries became more reliably happy events.

Exercise

The Speaker shares a Takeoff or a Reentry that has been challenging, or one that is regularly challenging.

Speaker, ask yourself: is it when you get out of bed and your partner is still sleeping? Is it when your partner goes to work in the morning? Is it in the evening when one of you gets home and the other partner is watching TV or making dinner? Or is it when one of you goes on a trip and there's a longer separation? Tell your partner the feelings you experience during this Takeoff or Reentry. What could you or your partner do to make the transition point smoother?

The Listener's role is to remain open to the Speaker's experiences even if they conflict with the Listener's own memory of the events.

Sample Exchange:

SPEAKER: I have a hard time with Takeoffs, especially the small, ordinary ones. When you get out of bed in the morning without reaching out to give me a hug, I feel lonely. If, on top of that, you leave the house without a face-to-face goodbye, just saying, "See you, I'm off!" from another room, I feel sad. But if you cuddle or we have a warm, face-to-face goodbye before you leave, I feel loved and relaxed. It helps me start my day out on the right foot.

LISTENER: Thank you for telling me about your challenges with some of our Takeoffs and Reentries. I want to be more sensitive to the ways we transition into and out of the space of our relationship.

15

Appreciations and Gratitude

Candace and Sean, in their late fifties, came in expressing a desire to feel closer. They were both dog lovers and had two Jack Russell Terriers—Jack and Jill—whom they sometimes referred to as "our kids." Candace worked as an IT contractor and Sean was a retired school counselor. Within a few minutes of arriving at my office, they were arguing.

Candace wanted to sit in the chair on the left, but Sean had a crick in his neck from sleeping in an awkward position the previous night. He wanted to sit in the same chair as Candace in order to face me without discomfort. Candace agreed to give up the desired chair if she had to, but only after giving Sean unsolicited advice on how to avoid cricks in his neck by engaging in activities other than compressing their living room couch. When Candace sat in the other chair, she mentioned the chill in my office and her proximity to the air conditioner. Sean finally agreed to take the chair on the right but wagged his finger at Candace for leaving her sweater in the car despite the fact that she always got cold.

We turned off the air conditioner and repositioned the chairs, and finally everyone was comfortable. But the real issue wasn't as easy to address as flipping a switch or moving furniture. For Sean and Candace, negativity, a focus on problems, and subtle complaining had become go-to strategies for voicing needs and trying to get the care and attention they craved from one another. Dissatisfaction permeated their lives and the toll it took was palpable.

Well-known relationship researcher, author, and public speaker John Gottman, PhD, has done studies that prove what he calls the 5 to 1 Rule. For every negative interaction between a couple, it takes five positive interactions to counterbalance it.

There's a simple technique I learned in my Imago Relationship Therapy certification training over a decade ago that I use with couples before every session. It involves sharing an appreciation for one another before sharing anything else that might be on their minds. Connecting with what we value in our partner is one way of consciously giving and receiving love. It sends an "all clear, we're safe" signal to the small, overworked section of the brain that is perpetually scanning the environment for signs of threat or danger.

When I encouraged Candace and Sean to begin our work together with an appreciation, they seemed perplexed. Sean winced as though the crick in his neck was acting up in a new location and Candace shivered even though the air conditioner was off.

"I can do it if you want, but it's going to sound phony," Candace said.

"I'm bad at sugarcoating stuff," Sean ventured.

"Okay, it's a bit of the 'fake it till you make it' strategy we're using here," I admitted, well aware this wasn't the most evidence-based intervention I'd ever made.

Sean said, "Fine. I have an appreciation. I appreciate you finally remembering to tidy up the kitchen after you got home late last night and made a huge mess."

Candace said, "And I'm grateful that after all these years, you finally started getting up early enough to walk our kiddos yesterday instead of sleeping in late while they cried and whimpered outside your door with their poor bladders ready to explode."

Sean and Candace weren't used to giving each other "clean" gratitudes. Their appreciations—laced with judgments and topped off with barbed finales—were self-defeating. This type of gratitude is what I call a "reverse sh*t sandwich" (definitely not the clinical term). There's a kernel of good inside it, but it's surrounded by unpalatable negativity.

Candace, Sean, and I spent a good part of our first session stripping down their RSSes until they were truly clean and positive expressions of gratitude.

Plenty of research has shown that as human beings, we have what's called a "negative survival bias," a wired-in biological tendency to focus on what's wrong in our environments. A thousand years ago, this bias helped us hear the crack of a twig that signaled a wildebeest in the underbrush. In our modern-day world, far from wildebeests, when we focus on cricks in our necks and chills in the air to the exclusion of the good in our relationships, it's high time for our negative survival bias to be counterbalanced with gratitude.

Exercise

The Speaker shares aspects of their partner that they value, including one physical characteristic, one personality trait, and a behavior. Make sure the appreciations are free of any RSS negativity, hidden blame, or judgment. Speaker, tell your partner how it feels to appreciate them. Does appreciation shift your view of the relationship, even if only slightly?

The Listener focuses on relaxing, keeping their posture open, and noticing how it feels to fully receive a compliment without deflecting or dismissing it. Do mental stories hijack your attention? Do you get jittery or go numb? Simply breathe, when you're the Listener. If tension arises, notice it and continue focusing on taking in your partner's words.

Sample Exchange:

SPEAKER: I admire your beauty, inside and out. I really respect what an incredibly loyal friend you are to the people you care about in your life and how close you are to your family. I love that when I was stressed out yesterday, you sat next to me, put your arm around me, and told me I was doing a great job painting the bathroom. Appreciating you reminds me what a caring person you are and helps me relax.

LISTENER: Thank you for appreciating me. I'm taking in your words. It feels good.

stepping stone

TANDEM EMOTIONAL MOUNTAIN CLIMBING

Imagine the time you spend in your Couples Time Container as a form of tandem emotional mountain climbing. Your overarching goal—fighting less and strengthening your relationship—is the anchor that keeps the communication stable when things get wobbly. Remembering your job description in your role of either Speaker or Listener builds safety in your Couples Spot. The way you manage your communication with one another affects whether you reach your goal on a regular basis and how safe you are on the climb. When partners are able to contain their reactivity as they speak and listen—when they interrupt their relationship horror stories and take psychological ownership (see chapters 4 and 11)—their connection tethers them, remaining strong and intact. When partners get reactive with one another, it begins to fray.

If you find yourself reacting in your Couples Spot, unable to stay true to your role as either Speaker or Listener, let your partner know you want to stop the discussion for now in order to keep your climb safe. Take a break from the exercise and come back to it later.

Self-Esteem

— Inferiority and Superiority
  (Gerald & Luke)

— Reparenting Your Own Inner Orphan
  (Arjun & Susan)

> Inferiority and superiority are different sides of the same coin.

16

Inferiority and Superiority

Gerald and Luke, from chapter 10, were in the middle of a major rupture. Gerald had surprised Luke on the anniversary of their first date by showing up at his five-star restaurant where he was the executive chef. This was what Luke had wanted Gerald to do for months, but instead of making him feel special, the night had ended with both of them feeling aggravated and misunderstood.

Although Gerald was in his early fifties, Luke was his first serious boyfriend. Taking another person's feelings consistently into account was a new and unfamiliar experience for him.

"I don't get it," Gerald said. "I do what you ask for, I pay you a visit and brag to everyone that you're my boyfriend. Isn't that what you wanted?"

"You flirted with the bartender half the night."

"I'm a flirt," Gerald said. "What can I say?"

"The whole point was to support me," Luke said coolly, staring at his fingernails. "To make me feel special. Not sit at the bar talking to someone else the whole night."

"You were busy," Gerald said. "You were in the kitchen the whole time bossing people around." I sensed that Gerald had started this sentence as a joke, but by the time it was out of his mouth, the sting of it rang true for them both.

Although both Gerald and Luke exuded style and success, they also both struggled with low self-esteem. This fragility was beginning to show up in their conflicts. Gerald hid his inadequacy under a front of grandiosity. Luke had a different tactic: He collapsed into feelings of inferiority. When he felt rejected or overwhelmed, he saw himself and his future as hopeless and lay in bed for days at a time.

"Now you're going to be miserable and it'll be my fault," Gerald said dramatically. "I'm always the bad guy."

"How did you feel at Luke's restaurant?" I asked Gerald. "You said Luke was busy."

"Me? I felt fine," Gerald said. "Out of place, but fine."

"Out of place?" I asked.

"It's his world, not mine." Gerald waved at Luke. "You're the star at the restaurant. If it were my old penthouse office back in the day, it would have been a different story. I was the king there."

His voice dipped and caught in his throat.

"The king," I repeated. From the way he'd said the word, it seemed like there might be more to it for him. "What does it mean, when Luke's the star or the king in his world?"

"He gets all the attention," Gerald said flatly. "But it's actually fine with me, I'm used to that happening. I've been in that position before with my brother."

Gerald's older brother had been a champion wrestler. His father's life had revolved around taking his eldest son to practices, signing him up for meets, and driving him to professional wrestling tournaments. Gerald had never felt like he could hold his father's attention. Gerald's mother was a former pianist who tutored kids in their home and was consumed with her students. Gerald hadn't been athletic or interested in piano, so he found attention elsewhere: He ended up spending a lot of time outside, befriending neighborhood kids and charming other people's parents into letting him stay over for dinner.

As an adult, Gerald found many ways of holding people's interest. He prided himself on his looks and his wealth. He had the best of everything: private jets, multiple houses, luxurious parties in the south of France. He socialized with people who reflected or confirmed his specialness, like the naked emperor in the story who was said to be wearing the finest clothes. Looking good and having the best of everything was a way of feeling valuable and worthy of attention.

Touching on what he'd felt as a 10-year-old boy, at the height of his brother's wrestling stardom, took many false starts and unfolded gradually, in bits and pieces. Acting as a stand-in for Gerald's father in a protocol Imago therapists call the Parent-Child Dialogue, Luke asked the 10-year-old Gerald questions about how it felt to live in his brother's shadow, how he coped without ever getting enough attention, and what he would have needed from him as his father to feel valued and loved. In the role of his 10-year-old self, Gerald managed to give a voice to some of the hurt he'd felt at going unnoticed in his family for so long. Luke validated him after the role play.

"I can see how you must have felt ignored when you came to my restaurant, like all the attention was on me. You probably felt that same lonely feeling you grew up with."

For Gerald, seeing Luke as an ally rather than a competitor meant working to acknowledge feelings of inadequacy and inferiority. Superiority was a smoke screen.

Exercise

The Speaker takes a moment to share their history with self-esteem.

Speaker, ask yourself: Did I grow up with low, high, or balanced self-esteem? When situations triggered inadequacy, what were some of the ways you coped? Have you ever tried to make up for low self-esteem by proving you were "better" or "the best"? Or did you withdraw emotionally and convince yourself that you were "the worst"?

Listener, bring mindfulness to maintaining a respectful and warm demeanor. It may not be easy for the Speaker to share about their self-image difficulties.

Sample Exchange:

SPEAKER: Growing up, I thought of myself as someone with high self-esteem. I worked hard to look perfect and pretty. I felt happiest whenever anybody complimented me. After I developed an eating disorder, I saw a school counselor and realized I actually had low self-esteem. I'd just always taken for granted that looks and accomplishments were everything. It's taken me a while to learn to value myself for who I am and to stop competing with other women and comparing myself to them.

LISTENER: Thank you for sharing your self-esteem challenges with me. I can see how it's important to recognize where you cover up feelings of inadequacy with feelings of superiority.

17

Reparenting Your Own Inner Orphan

A baby affects all areas of a couple's life. Arjun and Susan, from chapter 2, were slowly making peace with this reality. Ever since Kali's birth, Susan had been out of sorts, impatient and irritable. Motherhood was a radically different experience than she'd expected it to be.

"You're not getting enough sleep," Arjun said, trying to reassure her.

"That's not it," Susan insisted. "When I was writing my thesis as a graduate student I never slept, and I wasn't irritable then. I was in a great mood for months at a time."

"I can do more," Arjun offered. "I have vacation time. I can stay home when you need me to, or leave work early. You know how much I love taking care of Kali and being a dad."

That suggestion seemed to upset Susan even more.

"I can take care of Kali by myself," she snapped.

The degree of selflessness required to attend to a newborn, the loss of freedom, and the shift that comes with a whole new identity—all of this can be very different from the peace and fulfillment projected by beatific, smiling mothers on the covers of parenting magazines. When Susan was hard on herself for not being as happy as she was "supposed" to be, I gave her facts.

"Up to 20 percent of new moms experience postpartum depression. Irritability is completely normal. Sleep deprivation is a form of torture, and new moms don't sleep much. However you look at it, motherhood's a big change, and change is hard."

"I have a lot of strong emotions these days," Susan admitted. "I want Arjun's help with Kali because I'm exhausted, but when I think of him rocking her to sleep, it upsets me. I'm ashamed to say it but I think I'm jealous of her."

Arjun's eyebrows knitted together. Luckily, he'd gotten into the habit of containing his questions and concerns when Susan spoke, which allowed her to feel safe sharing more.

"If this feeling of jealousy were a portal in a time machine, where would it take us in your past? Does it connect to anything you experienced growing up?"

"Being eight and my parents coming home from the hospital with my baby brother," Susan said without hesitation. "When he was born, they ignored me. My dad was over-the-moon happy about having a son. We lived in the suburbs by then, they weren't as stressed out anymore, so my little brother got the best of them."

When Arjun delighted in his daughter, it reawakened Susan's own terror of being displaced. The flare-ups of jealousy and resentment she felt toward Arjun and Kali were remnants of the suffering she'd experienced witnessing her father bonding with her baby brother.

Many therapy models support clients in emotional processing by reconnecting them with buried, suppressed, or unconscious emotional experiences. Often, these experiences can be accessed by connecting clients with younger parts of themselves. Internal Family Systems, developed by Richard Schwartz, PhD, founder of Center for Self Leadership, looks at each individual person as containing within them multiple "parts" with distinct functions. Left to their own devices, these parts can operate in harmful ways even when their underlying psychological function is meant to be protective.

With Susan, we incorporated aspects of parts work and systems theory. We identified the jealous part of Susan as coming from her "inner orphan." This neglected child part had felt replaced by her baby brother. Speaking as her own eight-year-old self, Susan could voice her jealousy, fear, and grief safely. We identified the part of Susan that micromanaged Arjun and denied her jealousy as her "pseudo adult." The part of Susan bringing consciousness to all of this, and making better choices, we called her "true adult." Susan's true adult was the woman in the therapy room who was developing more self-awareness and a wider array of relational skills.

Susan found ways to connect compassionately to her "inner orphan" and respond to situations from her "true adult" rather than from her "pseudo adult." When Kali triggered anger or jealousy, Susan asked Arjun to take over parenting duties. She then wrote in a journal, meditated, or closed her eyes and imagined wrapping her own arms around a vision of herself as an eight-year-old child. As she reparented her own "inner orphan," Susan became a better, more conscious, and more compassionate mother to her actual daughter.

Exercise

Take two minutes to fill in the following worksheet, identifying a situation in the past when you felt triggered and circling two or three of the reactions and/or responses that most apply to you for each of the three figures that follow.

The Speaker shares their worksheet with their partner and talks about one thing they learned.

Sample Exchange:

SPEAKER: My situation is when you and I went dancing last weekend and I refused to dance. I blamed you for your choice of venue. I feared judgment. I learned that I sometimes mistake my pseudo adult for my true adult. My pseudo adult is rigid and fearful, but my true adult trusts life to work out and can let go of control.

I also learned that my inner orphan longs to play, feel joy, and express herself creatively. I need to engage my true adult to trust and surrender.

LISTENER: Thank you for sharing some of what you've learned about your inner orphan, your pseudo adult, and your true adult with me.

Inner Orphan Diagram and Worksheet

Situation _____

(e.g., when you don't call to tell me you'll be late)

INNER ORPHAN

- Fears abandonment
- Fears danger
- Fears engulfment
- Fears judgment
- Fears vulnerability

- Longs for connection
- Longs for freedom to play
- Longs for acceptance
- Longs for safety
- Longs for understanding

PSEUDO ADULT

- Reacts by blaming others
- Reacts by taking too much responsibility
- Reacts with complacency
- Reacts with controlling behaviors

- Reacts with defenses/ defensiveness
- Reacts with self-blame
- Reacts with withdrawal
- Tries to escape/avoid responsibility

TRUE ADULT

- Responds by using his/her authority/voice
- Responds by valuing self and others
- Responds with appropriate limit-setting
- Responds with compassion

- Responds with appropriate trust
- Responds with appropriate vulnerability
- Responds with confidence
- Responds with responsible action

stepping stone
THE HUDDLE

My son loves playing football with my husband and me in our front yard. When he's quarterback and I'm on his team, he begins each play with a huddle and shares his ideas in a conspiratorial whisper, tracing our moves on the textured, brown surface of the ball he's holding in the space between the two of us.

These moments before a play are the time when we solidify our alliance. We lean in close to one another, work together, and connect around a shared sense of purpose. It's exciting to be in it together, whatever happens.

Practice a huddle mind-set with your partner. Get physically and emotionally closer. Lean in. Work, plan, and share. You're allies. It's easy to overlook your alliance when you're caught up in daily tasks, roles, and routines. More important than the short-term success of any particular "play" you make is the huddle itself. It's that space you create together when you step out of your comfort zone and begin to get some skin in the game.

Life Philosophy

— Different Values
  (Shawntall & Logan)

— Scarcity and Abundance
  (Candace & Sean)

Values are the cardinal directions of your couples' compass.

18
Different Values

Logan scheduled a couples session because he and his fiancée Shawntall were considering calling off their wedding in two months.

"We're like strangers," Logan said during our initial phone call, his voice pained. The next day, when they entered my office, Logan shook my hand vigorously, thanking me for seeing them on such short notice. He exuded warmth and good humor. Shawntall slipped into an armchair, glancing around the room with a wan smile.

"I think this may be the first time we're actually spending 90 minutes together since we got engaged," Logan said, his tone falsely cheerful.

Shawntall rolled her eyes.

"Because now that we're engaged"—she raised her hand and mock whispered in my direction—"I need to put on a little white apron and give up my political career."

"Here it comes, death by a thousand cuts," Logan countered.

Humor can be an adaptive response to stressful situations and events, but in Logan's case, the jokes felt defensive.

"I'm sure you're aware that jokes and humor can cover up other feelings we don't always express," I pointed out bluntly as they settled in. "What do you think? Are there any feelings underneath the joking you're both doing right now?"

"With all due respect," Logan said, "saying I'm sad and crying about it won't cure me."

Shawntall clucked her tongue as she shook her head.

"See? That's the problem. How do you know? Maybe it *will* cure you to admit you're sad. You never talk about anything without joking."

"Fine," Logan said. "What I feel under the humor is lonely. But . . ."

"But . . ." Shawntall made a face.

"I fully support you! I'm insanely proud of what you're doing. You're incredible. Do you know what this woman does?" he asked me.

I shook my head, smiling. His admiration for Shawntall was contagious.

"Yale offered her a professorship last week," he said. "The problem is, I barely see her; she's too popular. She's always busy, always working late."

"Well, I respect you finally admitting you feel lonely instead of making light of it," Shawntall said. "When you joke about stuff like that it annoys me."

Both Logan and Shawntall valued love, friends, family, and having fun. During the courtship period of their relationship, they'd spent every night together, talking for hours, going to concerts, traveling to the beach and having all kinds of interesting and exciting sexual encounters. But since the wedding preparations began, Shawntall's political career had taken off and there were more demands on her time.

"I'm just not sure we want the same things anymore." Logan looked somber.

"You're oblivious, sometimes," Shawntall said, her tone affectionate but with an edge. "You see things through your white-guy lens. I have to call it like it is. I know you try, but you really don't get the extent of what I do or why it's so important."

"Does *everything* have to be political?" Logan said.

"If you'd been born in my skin, you'd know why everything has to be political," Shawntall said pointedly, raising an eyebrow.

Both Logan and Shawntall's values were linked to their gender and racial identities, to the realities of the worlds and communities they'd been raised in and still lived in today, and to their histories, which extended into the past long before they were born.

"Let's use this as a starting point," I suggested, handing Logan and Shawntall the Values Compass. We began discussing their own distinct values and how these connected to their sense of purpose, their life goals, and how they viewed themselves.

For Logan, fitness, partnership, and sexuality were indispensable values. For Shawntall, who had started focusing more on activism as well as her relationship to Logan, career, contribution, and creative freedom were becoming nonnegotiable values.

"We seem to have a bit of a discrepancy here," Shawntall noted.

Shawntall and Logan moved in together but decided to postpone their wedding. By identifying the values that were most important to them, they could make sense of the tension that arose from prioritizing different values at this point in their relationship. In six or eight months' time, they hoped to have a better idea of whether marriage was the right choice moving forward. Getting clear on their values recalibrated their expectations.

Exercise

Look at the Values Compass on the next page, circle your top three values and make note of your top value. Mark where you believe you are when it comes to living each value on the graph.

The Speaker discusses their top values. How does your partner support you in your values? If you could be anyone in the world for one day, who would it be? How do they embody your values?

Sample Exchange:

SPEAKER: My top three values are wealth/money, love/partnership, and fitness/physical health. My top value is wealth/money. My family always told me I should marry a doctor if I wanted to amass wealth, but I ended up going to business school and learning about finance. More women need to manage wealth and get competent at financial planning, because we can change the world that way. I feel supported in my value of wealth when you ask me questions about our investments.

If I could be anyone in the world for a day, it would be Donna Morton, entrepreneur, TEDx speaker, and the cofounder of First Power. I admire her outspokenness and her integrity in combining economics with the larger moral issues of our day, such as social justice and climate change.

LISTENER: Thank you for sharing your values with me. I appreciate knowing more about your values, and how they give your life a deeper meaning and purpose.

THE VALUES COMPASS

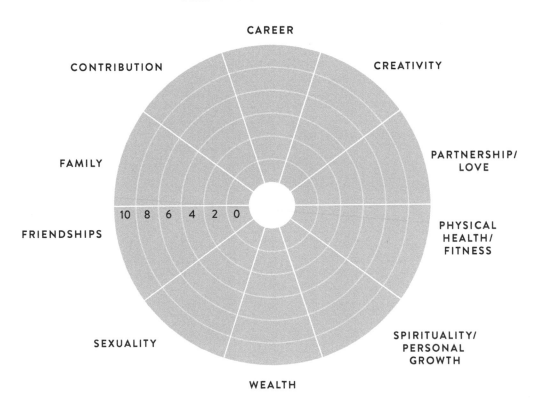

19

Scarcity and Abundance

"We've always had different mind-sets," Candace said, referring to her husband, Sean (see chapter 15). "He's afraid I'm getting too pink and fluffy in my outlook."

Sean was someone who saw dangers and risks. He doubted and questioned. He focused on negative potentials, on what wasn't there, on absences and deficiencies and how to mitigate them. Candace, on the other hand, saw possibilities and took positive results for granted. Her favorite catchphrase was, "Everything will work out."

This isn't uncommon. Members of a couple often have different mind-sets. The same prospect may feel exciting to one partner and scary to the other. Troubles only begin when these mind-sets become polarized.

In our culture, cultivating an "abundance mind-set" has recently become idealized as a panacea to a wide array of psychological and material ills. Whether it's cancer or poverty or a tragic circumstance, "think positive" can be the subtext of well-intentioned advice or suggestions. Scarcity thinking, in turn, tends to be viewed as negative and undesirable.

This bias plays out as the abundance-mind-set partner in a couple dismisses or rejects the scarcity-mind-set partner's perspective. In fact, Sean's "half-empty" perspective had proven useful many times: He remembered passports when they traveled, kept the gas tank full, and made sure the stove was off when they left the house. Candace didn't think about what could go wrong. She jumped headfirst into life, often without checking the ripcord of her parachute.

Relationships benefit from different perspectives and contexts: from seeing reality in a variety of ways. If Candace sees the proverbial glass half-full but is also able to borrow Sean's half-empty lens, her perspective includes a more reality-based shade of abundance. And if Sean sees the glass as half-empty but can step outside of his limited perspective to acknowledge Candace's view, his vision becomes more balanced and nuanced. The Ebbinghaus illusion, an optical illusion named after Hermann Ebbinghaus, the 19th-century German psychologist who created it, can be used to illustrate this point. A blue circle surrounded by several large gray circles appears smaller than a blue circle surrounded by smaller gray circles. In fact, both blue circles are the exact same size but the way they're perceived is influenced by the context of the circles around them.

For Sean and Candace, how they perceived the same "blue circle"— whether it was an investment opportunity, a new restaurant, or a parking ticket—depended on their viewpoints. Because "perception filters" are shaped by a unique blend of individual experiences, fears, needs, and hopes, there's a benefit in acknowledging the value of different views. The scope of what's perceived enlarges.

"But I really want Sean to see the glass half-full," Candace admitted. "I feel like we'd enjoy our lives so much more if he relaxed and trusted the universe to take care of things."

"How about you guys trade places briefly, as an experiment," I suggested. "Candace, you're Sean. Tell us the benefits of seeing the glass half-empty."

Candace leaned forward and assumed Sean's gruff facial expression.

"I'm prepared when things go wrong. Sometimes, because I'm thinking about it ahead of time, I actually prevent things from going wrong. I'm competent. I'm ready for whatever life throws in my direction. I'm not blindsided or shocked like other people."

"That was good," Sean said, pleased. "Plus, you're right."

"It's your turn to be Candace now, Sean," I said. "Glass half-full benefits . . . "

"Okay, I can do this." Sean leaned forward. He squared his shoulders and assumed a sweet, receptive facial expression that was spot-on as Candace. "If you think like me, you can relax and be in the present moment. I'm not worried. I have faith. I know how to enjoy life. Every day is a gift."

Candace was beaming.

"I never knew you could act," she said. "That was sweet."

"Both of your approaches have something to offer," I stated redundantly.

Judging from their smiles, they were convinced, at least for now.

EBBINGHAUS ILLUSION

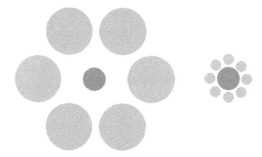

The two blue circles are exactly the same size; however, the one on the right appears larger.

Exercise

The Speaker talks about which mind-set they identify with most: abundance or scarcity. Avoid placing value judgments on either of these stances: Both have advantages and disadvantages. Talk about the pros and cons of how you see things. Share with your partner who or what you think most shaped your viewpoint. What are your fears of assuming or seeing the opposite viewpoint when you and your partner want different things?

Sample Exchange:

SPEAKER: I tend to have more of an abundance mind-set. The advantage is that I feel positive. The disadvantage is that sometimes I expect happiness and success to fall in my lap. What most shaped my glass-half-full viewpoint was seeing my parents always struggling to make ends meet. I ended up living in a dream world to try not to get sucked into their pessimism and anxiety. I refused to see life like that. What I fear about the glass-half-empty lens is that if I see things that way, I'll just give up and lose hope.

LISTENER: Thank you for sharing more about your mind-set and where it comes from.

stepping stone
INFINITE UNIVERSES

Vital relationships are ever-expanding universes, always presenting new wonders. Have you ever looked up at the night sky and seen a few stars? How many stars you see will depend on whether you're looking at the sky out in the wilderness or looking from your rooftop in a city. What we see in our partnership depends on the circumstances around us that influence what we're able to perceive at that moment. When your relationship isn't safe—when you're reactive or struggling with emotional survival issues that make it hard to attune to yourself and your partner—it's the equivalent of emotional light pollution. The lack of safety in your relational universe limits not only what you can notice and acknowledge, but also what you can appreciate and receive with wonder and awe. As you build safety through awareness, Love Rituals, communication skills, psychological ownership, and other tools and practices, you'll see more of what's really shining through your relationship.

It's an infinite universe, continually expanding.

Social Styles

— Extrovert, Introvert, or Ambivert
(Randy & Felice)

— Relationships with Friends
(Dale & Genevieve)

Know your partner's
social needs and how
to support them.

20

Extrovert, Introvert, or Ambivert

Few people would have guessed that Randy and Felice (see chapter 13) had trouble socializing. It was easy to imagine them dressed to the nines, moving through a crowd holding matching champagne flutes, rescuing awkward dinner conversations with grace. Over the 10 years of their marriage, they'd honed their skills at government functions and charity fundraisers. Randy, with his silver hair and wry smile, effortlessly combined new-world style with old-world charm. Felice's sincerity added depth to conversation.

   The problem was, Randy and Felice didn't like to socialize together. Randy felt wary of Felice's expectations of him when they were in public and was fearful of her inevitable post-party emotional hangovers. Although he liked having Felice by his side, he tended to forget about her when he got involved in a stimulating debate. He approached social events like a bungee jumper, taking solo leaps and getting intense rushes and hits of stimulation and attention.

Felice was insecure around people, a social weakness she'd learned to disguise well. She longed for Randy to check in with her when they were in social situations, to stay curious about her mental and emotional state, and to demonstrate his attunement through attentive gestures. But Randy shined his light so brightly in groups that it seemed to blind him to Felice's existence, even when she was standing right next to him.

"The only reason I socialize with you is because it's part of the 'government wife' job description," Felice said. "Otherwise, I would have stopped going to your events years ago."

"I know you hate it." Randy sounded bitter.

This couple's social challenges required openness to exploring their different needs: Randy thrived on feeling free, whereas Felice needed a trusted bond to feel grounded. As Randy sought to get his need for freedom and exploration met without supporting Felice socially, it intensified her insecurities. When she complained, Randy just got defensive and ended up distancing himself and shutting down.

Extroversion and introversion were first coined by the Swiss psychoanalyst Carl Jung as two ends of a spectrum related to social styles. In our session, we used these basic social-style formulations to begin framing Randy and Felice's social needs. Randy claimed he'd always felt like an extrovert. Socializing recharged him like a battery. He needed to be around people.

"Sometimes I'm extroverted," Felice said, "sometimes I'm introverted."

Travis Bradberry and Jean Greaves, coauthors of *Emotional Intelligence 2.0*, talk about the neurochemistry of sociability. Introverts tend to have more "dopamine-fueled" stimulation in their brains, while extroverts have less. Because the "feel-good" hormone dopamine drives sociability, the authors claim, full-on introverts—starting with higher levels of dopamine-fueled stimulation from the get-go—feel much more easily overwhelmed in social situations.

Extroverts have a very different experience. They actively seek out that same dopamine rush that introverts avoid.

"There's another term: 'ambiversion,'" I offered. "Most people fall somewhere in this ambiversion zone, somewhere between extroversion and introversion. Ambiverts have characteristics of both extroverts and introverts, depending on the situation."

"I can relate to that," Felice said.

I invited Felice to come up with three specific and doable requests for Randy. This is the basis of an Imago therapy tool known as the Behavior Change Request Dialogue. I used the acronym SMART as a reminder for Felice to create Specific, Measurable, Attainable, Relevant, and Time-Limited requests, setting Randy up to succeed in meeting her social needs by letting him know exactly what she wanted from him socially. Felice came up with three new behavioral opportunities for Randy to consider at the next social event they attended together. They were: 1) Within five minutes of our arrival, look me in the eye and say, "I see you and I appreciate you for being here," 2) 45 minutes after we arrive, tell me, "I'm happy to call you a car if you're ready to go," 3) Every 15 minutes, take my hand and hold it for 10 seconds before releasing it.

The concepts of extroversion and introversion weren't new to Randy and Felice, but exploring their different reactions to people in social situations allowed them to move into a more collaborative approach to socializing.

Exercise

The Speaker shares their answers to the following questions about their social style: How do I prefer to socialize? What makes me feel comfortable and uncomfortable socially? What impact do I think this has on my partner? Does it affect us socializing together, and if so, in what ways? Be careful to stay rooted in your own experience. Share your feelings with your partner as best you can, and, as always, be mindful of assigning blame or pointing fingers.

As the Listener, you're giving your partner space to share freely without commentary, even when you hear something you disagree with, or have an impulse to contradict, debate, or explain.

Sample Exchange:

SPEAKER: I prefer to socialize with one or two other couples over dinner, rather than at parties or concerts. I'm uncomfortable in big groups, especially when people are drinking. Alcohol used to change the dynamic in my family and lead to fights, so it scares me when you drink. I imagine you feel my judgment and don't like being controlled by me. This affects us because you like to drink in social situations and so you don't want to go out with me when there are other people involved. That hurts my feelings.

LISTENER: Thank you for sharing your preferences in social situations, for owning your feelings, and for seeing your contribution to some of our social tensions.

Healthy friendships
support a healthy
partnership.

21

Relationships
with Friends

Dale and Genevieve came into my office looking sullen and withdrawn.

Dale was a sociable, intense man. He worked as an executive chairman of a start-up company during the week. On weekends, he enjoyed spending his evenings relaxing with friends. Genevieve, on the other hand, spent her weekdays taking care of their eight-year-old daughter Lola and completing online courses as she worked toward her law degree. She liked spending weekends together as a family, with the occasional babysitter relieving her of her mothering duties so she could connect with Dale. Their different views of friendship had brought them to therapy.

"I'd like to talk about Jerry," Genevieve said in a soft voice soon after sitting down in my office. "And the woman he introduced you to last week."

"Nothing happened with her," Dale said, exasperated. "She sent me a flirtatious text and I deleted her number. You're focused on something that's a nonissue."

"You spent over four-hundred dollars at a strip club," Genevieve said quietly.

"That wasn't Jerry's fault," Dale snapped. "I drank too much. I shouldn't have been drinking."

"Genevieve, can you let Dale know your intention?" I asked. "Knowing what you want from him might help with how you talk about what happened."

"I want to get clarity and feel more trusting," Genevieve said.

I invited Dale to consider his intention as he listened to Genevieve share.

"How could you listen to her in a way that might help you stay open?"

"I'd like to see where you're coming from," Dale admitted.

Dale's friends meant the world to him. As a shy, overweight kid, he'd been teased a lot growing up and had often felt like an outsider. He'd endured a lot of bullying in elementary school. In high school, when he started to lose weight, he'd felt and acted more confident, and people had responded to him more positively. For the first time in his life, he'd experienced what it felt like to fit in socially.

Being treated like "one of the guys" had become the lynchpin of Dale's identity. Whenever Genevieve asked him to do things that implied taking a step back from his social world, or that might even temporarily set him apart from his friends, fears of being an outsider paralyzed him.

Genevieve, on the other hand, had been raised by her single father and a string of her father's younger girlfriends. Her mother had divorced her father when Genevieve was only five years old and returned to France. Genevieve had always struggled with trusting people she cared about. She was well aware that she'd learned to keep her distance from others as a protection against potential abandonment, but her awareness didn't make trusting any easier. She had to constantly remind herself that Dale loved her. She feared his outside relationships—with friends like Jerry—would ultimately divide them.

No More Fighting

As with all core conflicts, the fears underlying them had some basis in reality. Genevieve did exert control over Dale's friendships, and Dale was impressionable and over-accommodating with his close friends. He went along with others far too often, and at times doing so wasn't good for him. Even though his early circumstances had changed and he was no longer the shy, overweight kid who got bullied by his peers on the playground, he continued to choose conformity over integrity more often than he liked to admit. For this issue to present less of an emotional risk, Dale and Genevieve needed to change their approach to friendship.

With guidance, Genevieve took more psychological ownership (see chapter 11) for her challenges trusting people and risking closeness. She discovered that some of her judgment of Jerry had to do with wanting close friends of her own. She'd been placing all her intimacy needs on Dale as a way of avoiding having to confront her own fear of being rejected or left behind in her friendships. She began actively pursuing her own independent friendships, joining a local mom's watercolor workshop and an online Meetup group for runners. Dale started checking in with Genevieve more and letting her know what he was doing, even when he was out with his friends.

Exercise

The Speaker shares their beliefs and feelings about friendship. Are friendships important when you're in a couple? Have friendships hurt you or supported you? What role have friendships played in your life? Do you feel happy or relieved about your partner's friendships or do you sometimes feel jealous, threatened, or left out? Do you sometimes feel burdened by your partner's intimacy needs and wish they had more friendships to nourish and occupy them in their free time?

Sample Exchange:

SPEAKER: I was never good at making, keeping, or maintaining friendships. When I did make friends, I held on too tightly. My friends always seemed to want more distance from me than I wanted from them. I'm envious of how easily you make friends, and sometimes I feel insecure when you tell me that you're going out to dinner with your close friends or going away somewhere with them.

LISTENER: Thank you for sharing your perspective on friendships. I want to keep talking to you about what friendships mean in our lives and in our relationship, and how they impact us.

stepping stone

WHAT YOU NEED TO RECEIVE, I NEED TO GIVE

There's a beautiful symmetry in couplehood.

You might hear some people say that relationships are based on compromise, selflessness, or mutual self-sacrifice. In other words, some of our needs will align with some of our partner's needs, and the rest we'd better channel into other activities or simply make do without.

Others believe marriage is about taking turns. This theory posits that one of you will be selfless and generous now, and selfish and greedy later, and you'll trade back and forth. If you're lucky, at the end of the day, the giving and getting on your ledger sheets balances out and the exchange is equitable.

In fact, when it comes to the conscious, humbling work of couplehood, as two people go all-in, the ledger sheet dissolves. The line between "your needs" and "my needs" transforms. The needs of one person are related to the needs of the other in ways we may not immediately recognize, but, over time, an often surprising and powerful symmetry emerges. As you practice voicing your own needs and your partner finds ways to meet them, you are satisfied and uplifted, but your partner also transforms and grows into more of who they really are. Often, what our partners need us to give them connects with what we ourselves need to learn how to give in order to become the most complete, fully expressed version of ourselves.

Attachment Issues

— Excessive Dependence
(Elise & Mia)

— Counterdependency
(Barbara & Jordan)

— Unconditional Love
(Mary & John)

> Relationships aren't meant to meet all our needs; they're meant to expose them.

22

Excessive Dependence

Elise had begun individual counseling with me when she started dating Mia, a former colleague. Elise was half-Colombian, half-Jamaican, born and raised in Canada. Mia and Elise soon began seeing me as a couple. Elise had a habit of dating women who were in the process of stepping out of their heterosexual closets and who felt ambivalent about it. This was the case with Mia.

Mia was in love with Elise, yet she struggled with integrating the shift in self-concept and identity that came with owning her sexual identity and with the culture shock of taking in a new way of seeing the world. Mia had been married to her college sweetheart, a man she'd thought of as "my best friend" for 10 years. They'd lived a traditional suburban lifestyle, and even though she knew the life they'd been living wasn't right for her, she was also having trouble letting it go.

Elise described herself as a serial semi-monogamist. Her girlfriends overlapped. Her most passionate love affairs began with intense bonding, but she quickly became insecure and needy, requiring more reassurance than her lovers could give. Conflicts escalated. When the women she dated set boundaries with her, Elise's Dependency Distortions—her convictions about what was taking place at that moment with the person she depended on—locked in, blinding her to other ways of seeing the situation. Some of her Dependency Distortions were, "If I don't hold on tight, I'll lose my partner," "I need to control others or they'll leave me," and, "I have to be prepared for abandonment." These distortions triggered panic and she reacted by pursuing with even greater intensity, calling, texting, and demanding help, answers, love, or attention. Over time, when Elise sensed her latest love affair was nearing its end, she cultivated clandestine flirtations as a backup plan.

Elise had grown up on the outskirts of Toronto with her grandmother, who did her best to care for her but had severe fibromyalgia and was often strung out on prescription pills. Her own mother had returned to Colombia soon after she was born and died suddenly in a car accident. She'd never met her father. By the time Mia and Elise started dating, she already understood where her needy behaviors came from: She'd experienced more than her fair share of loss growing up, and she continued to fear losing people she depended on.

Elise and Mia broke up several times, and there was a lot of heartache as they struggled to find their way, individually and as a couple. During times of stress, Elise's clinging behaviors worsened, and Mia pulled away. Elise had a hard time reassuring and comforting herself when Mia wasn't around to support her. On a few occasions, Elise insisted Mia drop everything to prove she loved her, including the time when Mia took her son to Disney World and Elise insisted she come home from the trip early.

Through all of this, Elise resisted creating a backup plan with other women. In our work together, she realized that doing so was an unhelpful defense mechanism. Eventually Elise and Mia decided to separate. They reconnected after a few months and maintained a friendship. This was progress for Elise, who understood that historical events and forces had shaped her into the excessively dependent person she could become when she felt abandoned. She wanted to feel at ease with the inherent uncertainty in romantic relationships, to be able to soothe herself when she felt overcome by fear and self-doubt, rather than always looking outside of herself for comfort.

Elise decided to take a yearlong sabbatical from romance to care for her inner orphan (see chapter 17). She came to therapy once weekly for six more months, and then switched to once monthly, experimenting in her daily life with bringing more awareness and acceptance to her feelings while working on avoiding the pitfalls of old reactions and behaviors.

By the end of the year, Elise was still single, but for the first time in her life, she wasn't in a rush to join herself at the hip with a partner. She felt more confident in her ability to be alone, but also to give the person she committed to in the future the space that might allow them both to relax and breathe more easily.

Exercise

The Speaker talks about their experience of depending on others early on in their life. Who did you depend on most growing up? Talk about a time you depended on someone and they weren't able, for whatever reason, to be there for you. How did you cope? What did you believe about depending on others? (See the following Dependency Distortions.) What can you change about your Dependency Distortions and reactive behaviors to find more breathing room in your relationship?

Sample Exchange:

SPEAKER: I depended on my big brother. My parents were good people, but they were very busy trying to provide for us. One day, my brother had a friend over, and I asked them to play hide-and-seek with me. I remember waiting for a long time under a bed, but they never came looking for me. When I finally came out, my brother laughed and said, "Seriously? You thought we would play that stupid game with you?" I felt tricked and foolish. Some of my Dependency Distortions have been, "You can't trust people you love," and, "Be prepared for betrayal." One thing I can change is how much I criticize your friends because I'm afraid they'll influence you in ways that will divide us or separate us.

LISTENER: Thank you for sharing more with me about your early experiences with dependence. I'm glad you're willing to look at some of your Dependency Distortions and recognize behaviors that no longer serve you or us.

Dependency Distortions

- Be hypervigilant to keep others' love
- Be prepared for abandonment
- Be prepared for betrayal
- Be prepared to be hurt
- Hold on tightly to avoid rejection
- Control others or they'll leave you
- Work hard to keep someone's love
- Make others responsible for you so they won't leave you
- I need protection
- I need someone else to complete me
- I need someone to rescue me
- I need to be "good" and giving to keep others' love

Depending on no one leads to a loveless life.

23

Counterdependency

In the aftermath of Barbara's affair, Jordan called me because, in his words, "If I leave now, I'll never know what went wrong." A stately, beautiful woman in her late thirties, Barbara said her mother had been an Italian countess. She herself liked to dress regally, in floor-length skirts and silky, pastel blouses that contrasted with her black hair. Her long neck contributed to the impression that she was gazing down at everything, evaluating a world that was always falling ever so slightly short of her expectations. When we met, she avoided meeting my gaze and seemed indifferent and detached.

This was a façade. Barbara cared. She admitted during one of our sessions that she was certain I'd branded her with a scarlet letter because of her affair even before I'd met her. She was also afraid that she'd lost Jordan's heart forever and that even if they stayed together, he'd always view her with suspicion.

Jordan was a kind, intelligent, and handsome man of Eastern European descent who owned and ran a restaurant in Northwest Washington, DC. Barbara—a former model—made her living as a personal-style consultant. She and Jordan had already been dating for a year and begun talking about moving in together when he discovered she'd gotten romantically re-involved with one of her wealthy ex-clients. Part of what tormented Jordan was discovering that Barbara's ex-client had spent exorbitant sums of money on Barbara after their trysts, buying her expensive gifts, like diamond bracelets and designer handbags.

Barbara had been elusive and mysterious with Jordan. She waited till the last minute to agree to their dates. She rarely let him know her plans for the week. More than once, she'd given him contradictory information about her whereabouts. She would sometimes go days without responding to his texts or calls. Though Jordan wasn't typically jealous, with Barbara, he got anxious, started drinking more, and developed insomnia. Her behaviors fed into his fears.

"I worry I'm not successful enough for you," he told her. Jordan couldn't figure out whether Barbara was genuinely interested in being with him or just toying with his heart for her own entertainment.

Ironically, Barbara hadn't been certain about her level of interest in Jordan, either, until he was preparing to break up with her. Faced with the possibility of losing him, Barbara's attachment to Jordan took hold.

Barbara had grown up a latchkey kid. Her Italian countess mother had worked full-time as a flight attendant on Alitalia. Barbara had watched soap operas for years and fantasized about belonging to the families she saw depicted on TV. At fifteen, she'd learned to use her charm, biting humor, and beauty to her advantage. Although she was frequently depressed and anxious, she relied on the money she earned and the privileges her money bought her to feel better about herself. When Jordan entered her life, her old desire for family reawakened. The anxiety she felt when he wasn't with her reconnected her to the loneliness she'd lived with as a girl waiting for her mother to come home. Barbara craved closeness with Jordan but also feared it. What if she let herself love him and he left?

For Barbara, the affair with her former client had been one way of protecting herself from pain. By unconsciously behaving in ways that sabotaged her connection to Jordan, she was trying to save herself from the possibility of feeling helpless and vulnerable again, as she'd felt with her mom.

Independence is exalted in our culture. Neediness and interpersonal vulnerability are often pathologized and labeled "codependence." But there's another type of unhealthy dependence that is often overlooked: counterdependence. This is when a person decides to count on no one at all, or to carefully control their degree of attachment to important others in their life, usually as a way of protecting themselves in the wake of an old abandonment. It's exactly what I saw Barbara doing with Jordan. Many counterdependent individuals move through the world in a sparkling sonic boom of admiration, well camouflaged within their broad networks of friends, relatives and acquaintances. Their smiling, social media avatars are a collage of all the most sought-after trappings of success.

Being aloof and slightly out of reach seems to be in fashion these days, and close human relationships are one of the only places where counterdependency can be fully exposed for the problem it is. It wasn't until Barbara recognized why she was sabotaging the intimacy she longed for with Jordan that she could soften into accepting her desire to partner with him and risk getting hurt. Connecting with the intensity of her longing for family—and for family with Jordan—meant being vulnerable in a way Barbara wasn't used to. It was painful and difficult to open herself to the possibility of another's rejection. At the same time, aligning with her truth despite the risks gave her the courage to stop playing games and start loving for real.

Exercise

The Speaker talks about their experience of counterdependency. Which counterdependent tendencies from the following list have you noticed in yourself? Share an example. Explore your fear in that situation. What would be a more courageous, "interdependent" approach, if a similar situation were to arise today?

Sample Exchange:

SPEAKER: One of my counterdependent tendencies is to avoid asking people for support. When I was fired from my job last year, I felt depressed. Instead of calling my brother, I just pretended everything was fine. A more interdependent approach would have been to reach out to my brother, or to someone else I trusted, and tell them the truth. I know I do this with you, sometimes. I pretend I don't need your help when I really do.

LISTENER: Thank you for sharing this counterdependent tendency with me. It takes courage to recognize the ways you sometimes try to avoid depending on me and why.

COUNTERDEPENDENT TENDENCIES

- Avoiding asking for help
- Avoiding intimacy
- Avoiding rejection by rejecting first
- Avoiding vulnerability
- Complaining about neediness in others
- Distancing from your partner
- Falling "out of love" quickly
- Feeling trapped in partnership
- Highly sensitive to criticism
- Living with constant self-criticism
- Needing to win arguments
- Overly focused on self
- Perfectionistic
- Reacting to "happy" couples with cynicism
- Seeing relationships as transactions or power games
- Seeing weaknesses as shameful
- Struggling with tenderness
- Viewing all touch as sexual

24

Unconditional Love

Mary and John had been having a hard time as empty nesters. Mary said her goal was to "work on communication."

John phrased it differently: "I'd like to know what she wants. I honestly don't know what she expects from me half the time."

When Mary and John were raising their daughters, the busyness of parenting had diverted their attention away from the subtle but chronic dissatisfaction they'd felt in their marriage.

"I feel alone," Mary said. "A lot."

John worked as a hospital administrator. Mary was a retired teacher who now created necklaces and bracelets out of handmade glass beads, which she sold on Etsy. On weekdays, John left for work while Mary slept and came home at five in the evening, usually when she was out walking. At dinner, they talked briefly about their day. On weekends, John woke before dawn, ate breakfast, and disappeared into his home office.

"Sometimes, on Saturday morning, when you come downstairs, I can't tell whether you're venting or you want me to fix whatever you're talking to me about," John said. "I'd like to understand your priorities better so I know when you need me to listen to you."

"I wish you'd always listen," Mary said.

"I listen to people all week long," John said. "On weekends I want to chill out. But if I know something's important to you, I'll stop what I'm doing and try to pay attention."

"That's just it," Mary said with a tense smile. "Everything you're doing is always so much more important than listening to me. For something I say to be worth your attention, I'd probably have to tell you the house was burning down."

John tugged at one of his ears. His eyes glazed over.

I leaned toward Mary and suggested she repeat the following phrase: "What I really want when I come into your study is your full attention."

"It's true," Mary said. "What I really want is your full attention."

"And when I don't get your full attention, I feel . . ."

"Lonely," Mary said. "Unloved. I've felt that way for a long time now."

John looked confused.

I turned to John. "Did you ever just listen to your daughters?" I asked him. "Just because you loved them, for no real reason. Just because they were talking to you?"

John thought about this for a moment.

"I try to advise them a lot. But sometimes I do just listen. I guess I should do that more. They're great girls."

"Could you try to listen to Mary like that?"

All human beings need and crave unconditional love: that feeling of being valued for no big, fancy, logical reason, just for being you. This is what Mary hungered for and wasn't getting enough of from John.

In his book *Real Love*, Greg Baer, MD, traces conflicts between couples to a shortage of real love and an excess of what he calls "imitation love"—the strings-attached kind of love most of us know well. As we talked more, I learned that both Mary and John had grown up surrounded by *conditional* love. Mary had learned to stay in the good graces of her parents and teachers by behaving properly, keeping a low profile, and doing what was expected of her. John had secured the love of adults in his life by completing chores, getting good grades, and avoiding making mistakes as much as possible.

John and Mary began recalling instances when they'd felt unconditionally loved. It was an emotional experience for both of them to connect with these peak moments in friendships and family relationships, and sometimes with strangers who had valued them exactly as they were. They felt grateful, remembering the people who'd opened them up to this kind of love in the past. There was also grief at not having had more of these unconditionally loving experiences in their life.

We collaborated on GULPs—Give Unconditional Love Plans. GULPs targeted key moments in their days when there were opportunities to give each other unconditional love. John agreed to meet Mary's longing for unconditional love by greeting her with a smile when she entered his study. Mary agreed to show John unconditional love by asking him if she could bring him a cup of tea or a glass of water when he was immersed in a book. Such tiny steps can make a big difference. Mary compared the small moments of unconditional love that passed between her and John with the handmade glass beads she threaded carefully and thoughtfully together on a string to create her beautiful, one-of-a-kind, bracelets and necklaces.

Through recognizing their longing for unconditional love, and coming up with GULPs tailored to specific moments in their everyday lives, John and Mary increased their awareness of the daily opportunities that existed to love one another without conditions or expectations.

Exercise

Take two or three minutes and use the following sheet to formulate a GULP. The Speaker then shares their GULP and how it might feel to receive unconditional love in this situation.

Sample Exchange:

SPEAKER: One situation is when you're in a different room and you raise your voice and yell, "Hey, I can't close the window, help me!" or I'm going to the store and you call out, "Don't forget to pick up *x*, *y*, or *z*." When you do that, I feel unimportant and disregarded. What would feel unconditionally loving to me would be if you made an effort to stop what you're doing and then communicated with me face-to-face. That would help me feel happier, loved and more relaxed.

LISTENER: Thank you for telling me about this situation and for giving me the opportunity to practice giving you unconditional love.

Give Unconditional Love Plan (GULP)

Situation: (Driving somewhere together) _____

_____

_____

Key Moment: (I make a wrong turn) _____

_____

_____

Old Response: (Pointing out what I should have done) _____

_____

_____

Unconditional Loving Response:
("It's not a big deal, we all make wrong turns.")

_____

_____

_____

I'll Feel: (Loved, relaxed, supported) _____

_____

_____

stepping stone
MESSENGERS IN DISGUISE

Remember, your current struggles with your partner—whether mild or very distressing—are messengers in disguise. They're harbingers of change. Change may be scary, but the end result of not changing is often much scarier. By identifying areas of vulnerability in your relationship, practicing a range of communication skills, and strengthening your bond from week to week, you and your partner are choosing a conscious approach to change. Over time, and with practice, this work you're doing has the power to sustain your love.

When you notice negative emotions arising in your Couples Spot, try acknowledging these feelings silently to yourself with gentle phrases, like, "I see you," or, "Welcome, friend." You are speaking to the emotions themselves. It may feel odd, but acknowledging them instead of pushing them down or denying them can help your feelings do what they're here to do: flow and be felt by you. See if you can find some emotional space within you, focusing on your breath or counting slowly from one to three, and observe your feelings like the mix of oil and wax in a lava lamp. Our conflicts and our negative emotions have a place in our lives. They're messengers urging us to take care of ourselves, pay attention, speak up, and set boundaries.

Power and Control

— Gender Roles and Relationship Roles
(Dale & Genevieve)

— Shared Decision-Making
(Shawntall & Logan)

25

Gender Roles and Relationship Roles

Dale and Genevieve (see chapter 21) hadn't given their gender roles much thought. Dale had pretty much lived his life in accordance with standard, socially accepted markers of manhood and maleness. He watched sports, hung out with guy friends, avoided exhibiting too much emotion or showing physical affection in public, preferred not to ask for help or directions while driving, and tended to prioritize success and competence over vulnerability and intimacy. He followed stock market trends, liked music that spiked his adrenaline, and prided himself on fixing things.

Genevieve had a receptive, feminine style, and typically acted in ways that many of the women she knew and admired also acted. Like Dale, she also exhibited traits that were commonly considered gender-congruent in mainstream culture: She wasn't particularly ambitious, let Dale figure out the tip amount at restaurants, and threw herself wholeheartedly into caretaker roles, most noticeably with their daughter, Lola. Genevieve was soft-spoken, self-sacrificing, and more sensitive to interpersonal signals than Dale. She let him oversee their financial choices.

But when Dale lost his job, gender issues surfaced in unexpected ways.

Finding a new job proved difficult for Dale. Unemployment rates were soaring and there was a hiring freeze across the board in his city for the positions he was most qualified for. Dale had quit smoking when Lola was born, but after losing his job, he took long, brooding drives and came home smelling of cigarettes. Genevieve felt like she was walking on eggshells around him. They began arguing in front of Lola more frequently.

"I can't believe you're spending what little money we have on cigarettes," Genevieve said in one of our sessions. "Your father died of lung cancer. Do you want to get cancer, too?"

"Maybe that wouldn't be the worst thing," Dale said morosely. "I can't even provide for my family. What kind of a man am I? Nobody wants to hire me. I'm not marketable."

Dale's job loss, and the expectations he was putting on himself as the "man" of the family, had triggered a depressive episode. In addition to our couples therapy, he began seeing a psychiatrist, who prescribed an antidepressant and worked with me to keep an eye on Dale's depressive symptoms.

When Genevieve received an offer for a well-paying job from a local law firm, she accepted. Initially, this had seemed like a hopeful development; however, Dale's resentment increased as he took over more of Genevieve's prior parenting duties.

"Maybe I should start wearing your dresses and skirts, too, and put on an apron."

"Are you serious?" Genevieve asked. She covered her face with her hands. When she took them away, her eyes were red. "We're in the twenty-first century! Who cares which one of us is earning the money? We're a team. Your pride is destroying us."

"How does it feel that Genevieve goes to work while you take care of Lola?" I asked.

Dale looked sullen and angry. He shrugged.

"Not good," he said. "I feel like a failure. I feel worthless."

It wasn't easy for Genevieve to listen to Dale's self-judgment and expressions of inadequacy and shame without reacting. She had fears of her own: What if Dale's depression deepened? What if he became more overtly self-destructive? But it was essential to explore the impact of the role changes that were taking place in Genevieve and Dale's relationship, and to look at the gender role expectations they'd both grown up with. The more space we made to understand what was going on emotionally for them as their gender roles became increasingly fluid, the more Dale was able to release his shame and allow room for a new perspective.

A few months into Genevieve's new job, when Dale was getting Lola ready for school, he received a job offer from a well-respected tech company. When he told us about that moment later in one of our sessions, he said his own reaction had surprised him. Instead of feeling elated, he'd felt a sense of regret. When he'd called the company back, he'd accepted the offer under the condition that they grant him flexibility in the afternoons. Despite his depression and the feelings of failure that came with falling short of certain rigid gender role strictures he'd accepted for most of his life, Dale had learned that he genuinely *wanted* more time to do things at home and take care of Lola.

Dale got the job, and Genevieve reworked her morning schedule so she could arrive at her law firm later and take Lola to school. Dale continued picking his daughter up at the bus stop every day.

"I'm not sacrificing that moment for anything," he said, "Hearing Lola call out to her friends, 'That's my daddy,' with a huge smile on her face—that's priceless."

Exercise

The Speaker talks about what gender means to them. Do you identify wholeheartedly with the gender of the body you were born into? What did you learn about gender roles growing up? What have been some of the pluses of identifying with one or the other gender and what have been some of the minuses? If you could be a different gender for a day, what would you give yourself permission to experience?

Sample Exchange:

SPEAKER: I've always identified with being male, but I remember having a more fluid view of masculinity when I was a child. It included traits that now I see are associated with femininity, such as emotional sensitivity. I had two older sisters, and they would let me join in on their games and dress me up in wigs and paint my nails. But when I was six, my father said, "You're not a girl. Go play with Jackson," who was the neighborhood bully and the only boy my age on the block. I started believing boys and girls needed to play separately and couldn't be friends or share interests. If I could be female for one day, I'd give myself permission to hug and cuddle more. I crave touch, but I learned that as a man, it's weak to want touch that's not sexual.

LISTENER: Thank you for sharing what shaped your views about gender, and for thinking about expanding beyond that so we can really be ourselves.

Making decisions together reflects a true meeting of minds.

26

Shared Decision-Making

Collaborative decision-making had never been easy for Shawntall and Logan (see chapter 18). Despite having several boyfriends before Logan, Shawntall had lived alone since college, and she was used to her way of doing things. Logan's ex-wife—a young, timid religious woman that his Jewish parents had pressured him to marry—had been introverted and compliant. The decision-making responsibilities had largely fallen to him in that relationship. Logan had always wanted to be partnered with a strong woman who spoke her mind, but after three months of living with Shawntall, he was finding it challenging.

"I feel like the minute I suggest something, you shut it down," Logan said in one of our sessions. Shawntall observed him with a skeptical expression.

"Do you have an example?" I asked.

"When we went shopping for a couch last weekend," Logan said, "I suggested the sectional. And you just reacted with, 'Over my dead body.'"

"I didn't know couches meant so much to you," Shawntall said.

"That's not the point. It's about deciding together."

Logan had grown up with wealthy, perfectionistic parents who rarely gave him the freedom to make—and learn—from his own decisions and mistakes. When Shawntall didn't make the effort to hear him out or allow him to weigh in on things—even simple things like the type of couch they bought—he felt the same way he had with his mom and dad: angry, controlled, and unseen.

Shawntall, on the other hand, had taken on an excess of responsibilities early in her life. Her father had been diabetic, and Shawntall had made sure he took his insulin and got to his doctor's appointments while her mother worked as a hospice nurse. She'd been making important decisions for her own parents from a young age. Because adults outside her family had frequently doubted and questioned her, she'd learned to speak up and push back.

"As a black girl, that was my reality," Shawntall said. "People in schools and doctor's offices were always giving me the message, 'Do as you're told and don't make a scene.' But I couldn't afford to do as I was told. My family depended on me."

What Logan needed from Shawntall wasn't agreement or acquiescence, though. He needed her to contain her negative reactions, even if she disagreed with him, and give his ideas some space to "float," even if just for a moment, as possibilities.

"I want you to hear my point of view," Logan clarified. "If you did, I would feel like you respect how I think and like my point of view matters to you enough for you to consider it."

"I can try, but that's going to be tough for me," Shawntall said, shrugging. "I call it like it is. You know that's just who I am."

Logan took a deep breath. "It's not that I want you to change who you are. I know you're opinionated, and I love that about you. But when it comes to making a choice together, I want you to consider that I might see something you don't see, and to be able to discuss the pros and cons. You could say, 'Oh, interesting, so you like the sectional couch. I would never have guessed that. Tell me why you think it's a good option,'" Logan offered.

"Even if I hate the couch?" Shawntall laughed. "Okay, I'll try. I *will* try."

Shawntall was willing to work on staying more open-minded, but in turn she needed something from Logan. "Instead of assuming I don't care about your input, can you say something like, 'Wow, you seem like you have a strong opinion about this. Why is this so important to you?'" She needed patience from him, even if she reacted negatively to one of his ideas. Shawntall thought it might also help if he said, "I trust your judgment, but I'd still like to weigh in on this decision."

If you're clear on what you want, making space to consider what your partner thinks can be difficult. There's an urgency to decision-making moments. If we "know" what would work best—whether it's the type of couch or the turn our partner needs to take off the highway—we assert ourselves and sometimes steamroll others' initiatives without even realizing what we're doing.

Collaborative decision-making is a practice in trust, acceptance, and humility. As couples, it can help to remember that there's something at stake in our decisions that's far more important than getting our way: our partner's sense of agency in the relationship, and their worthiness as reflected in our eyes.

Exercise

The Speaker describes the positive things about how they make decisions as a couple. Could you be more collaborative? When you and your partner disagree, or have different opinions regarding a decision, what do you need to remember to take your partner's view into account? What would you like your partner to remember?

Sample Exchange:

SPEAKER: I'm happy with how we make big decisions, like where to go on vacation or where to live. We talk things through and hear each other out. But on little decisions, like what movie to see or where to eat, we could do better. I often feel steamrolled into seeing movies I don't like and eating only where you want to eat. I don't mind seeing your movies, sometimes, or eating at restaurants you like, but then let's acknowledge it and take turns deciding. If I disagree with one of your decisions, I need to remind myself that I have to speak up instead of just swallowing my resentment. I'd like you to keep in mind that even though I do defer to you a lot, I still want you to consider my input.

LISTENER: Thank you for letting me know more about what it means to make decisions together, and what you need from me to keep our decisions collaborative.

stepping stone
COMPARE AND DESPAIR

Comparing the partner you *do* have to the imaginary or idealized partner you *don't* have is destructive. Social exchange theorists call this "Comparison Level for Alternatives," or CLalt, a relational phenomenon couples researcher and relationship expert John Gottman, PhD, talks about in a video clip called "How to Build Trust." When couples compare each other to the ideal partner "out there," or to a romanticized past partner, they're sabotaging their current relationship. At its worst, this can lead to a breakup partners regret.

Commit to noticing when you find yourself longing for exes, idealizing past romantic experiences, or daydreaming about fantasy lovers, then connect with the underlying feelings of loneliness, loss, or fear. Try counterbalancing the tendency to escape into an imagined or bygone reality by appreciating your partner. Once you complete the exercise at the end of chapter 47, you can make a practice of regularly going back to the relationship benefits you've circled or written down, and continue adding to the list.

Ruptures

— The Damage of Disrespect
  (Shane & Elena)

— Expressing Anger
  (Shane & Elena)

— Understanding Your Triggers
  (Shane & Elena)

How you
treat your partner is
a reflection of how you
treat your relationship.

27

The Damage of Disrespect

Shane and Elena were in trouble. Even as he lowered himself into the chair in my office, Shane held his body in what looked like a perpetual crouch, casting sidelong glances to the left and right with minimal head movements. It was as if he were simultaneously checking the fortifications of his bunker while preparing to fend off an attack. Elena sat across from him with her arms crossed. Hostility rose off her like radioactive gamma waves. When I asked about what had brought them to therapy, Elena looked at Shane and said, "We're here for our children."

"Our son's counselor recommended we see a therapist together," Shane muttered. "Our problems seem to be contributing to his behavioral issues at school."

Despite this book's aspirational title, if you're in a couple, some degree of fighting is likely to occur. I would even go so far as to say infrequent or moderate amounts of what I'll call controlled, "respectful" fighting where couples get emotional but without blaming each other can prove cathartic, or be mined for helpful information about triggers, leading to greater self-awareness. At the same time, it's probably no surprise to hear that negative patterns of relating, unchecked, can eat away at long-term closeness and well-being. Though negative patterns occur in the midst of fights, when couples are more reactive, avoiding conflicts and walking on eggshells because you're afraid of fights also inhibits closeness.

Relationship expert John Gottman, PhD, identified four negative patterns of interaction he calls "the Four Horsemen." This name is a reference to the Four Horsemen of the Apocalypse in the New Testament. Lovely stuff! Interestingly, Gottman has been able to predict (with a high degree of accuracy) which marriages will end in divorce based on the appearance of these four traits in a couple's interactions.

Gottman's Four Horsemen are Criticism, Defensiveness, Contempt, and Stonewalling.

The first—Criticism—involves focusing on your partner's perceived flaws and failings. One antidote to criticism Gottman offers is the use of "gentle startups"—warm, affectionate segues into potentially triggering conversations, observations, questions, or requests.

Defensiveness, Horseman two, is the negative pattern of deflecting a perceived attack by denying or counterattacking. Taking responsibility for your part in conflicts can work as an antidote to this pattern.

Contempt—Horseman three—uses mockery, sarcasm, outright name-calling, or shows of disgust to cast your partner as inferior. "Building a culture of appreciation" and overtly respecting your bond is one of Gottman's antidotes to this pattern.

Stonewalling is the fourth Horseman. Stonewallers withdraw emotionally and sometimes physically during an interaction. This can be the subtlest of the Horsemen and hard to recognize since the line between active stonewalling and reactive self-protectiveness sometimes blurs. Whereas the other Horsemen are recognizable in things people do and say, stonewalling is more about what someone *isn't* doing. Stonewallers "play dead" emotionally and psychologically. They don't react, they don't respond, they don't communicate, and sometimes they don't even make eye contact. Learning to recognize and respect signs of your own and your partner's psychological and emotional overwhelm and taking breaks from charged topics can give stonewallers the space they need to stay connected, regulate their emotions, and resume a discussion later.

I explained Gottman's theory of the Four Horsemen to Elena and Shane. Though they tended to be more conflict-avoidant than direct or confrontational, they agreed that they recognized the hoofmarks of the Four Horsemen all over their relationship.

"Would you be willing to identify the Horsemen you resort to most?" I asked.

Answering this question truthfully isn't easy. It takes courage to "out" our interpersonal ugliness and admit we throw aggressive or destructive adult tantrums disguised as self-righteousness, indifference, and even martyrdom. It can be doubly difficult to take responsibility when we suspect our partner may use our admissions against us.

"I stonewall," Shane said quietly, after a long moment of silence. "That's definitely something I do. You mentioned contempt can be a smirk or an eye-roll, so I guess I'm contemptuous, too. I'm kind of passive-aggressive."

Elena stared at Shane with a look of suspicion. Finally, she nodded.

"Thanks for admitting that," she said.

"I'm not proud of it," Shane said. "I want to change how I interact with you. It breaks my heart to think our kids are picking up on our negativity. I can see it's hurting them."

Elena's arms were still crossed over her chest, but there were tears in her eyes.

"What about you?" I asked her, hoping to keep the momentum going.

"I don't know," Elena said, reaching for a tissue. "I'm just sad."

Although she wasn't quite ready to show us around her stables and introduce us to the Horsemen she used in moments she wasn't particularly proud of, Shane's admission had clearly made an impression on her. He'd begun to change the culture of their relationship from one of blame to one of accountability.

Exercise

The Speaker identifies which of Gottman's Four Horsemen they ride with most frequently. Why do you think this particular Horseman will get you somewhere? Do you remember seeing others use this Horseman in your childhood? During high-conflict situations, if you could translate your Horseman into vulnerable, respectful language, what do you think you would say?

Sample Exchange:

SPEAKER: The Horsemen that I use most are Criticism and Contempt. I criticized you just yesterday for the way you were dressed because you were pleased with how you looked, and I showed contempt this morning when you told me about your award and I said, "Oh, you're such a good boy, you got an A at work." I think I use sarcasm and contempt as a way of trying to bring you down a notch or two when I feel left out or threatened. I'm afraid you'll think I'm inferior, or that you're too good for me. If I could translate my Horsemen into words, I'd probably say, "I feel vulnerable," or, "I'm afraid you'll leave me."

LISTENER: I'm grateful that you're taking responsibility for your negative communication patterns, making it safer for us to interact and be together.

> Anger isn't a problem, but avoiding or indulging it is.

28

Expressing Anger

Elena and Shane (see chapter 27) didn't really fight. Elena seethed, while Shane channeled his energy into maintaining an invisible emotional force field around him to ward off incoming verbal and energetic projectiles. In reality, they were both afraid of anger.

It wasn't until their eight-year-old son, Joseph, started getting into fistfights at school and their ten-year-old daughter, Rachel, showed signs of an eating disorder that this couple realized they might benefit from looking at how they managed and mismanaged their anger.

Ignoring anger doesn't make it disappear: like toxic waste buried under a pristine plot of land, it can seep into the water supply and wreak havoc on your mental, emotional, and physical well-being. Elena and Shane admitted they rarely fought and, in fact, avoided conflict.

"Maybe once or twice a year," Elena said hesitantly. "And when we do, it's bad."

A week before coming to counseling, Elena had been blindsided by her own rage. They'd been in the car on their way to a beach house. Elena had exploded, screaming at the top of her lungs, making negative comments about anything and everything she could think of related to Shane and their life together. Even Elena admitted the trigger had been minor—a dismissive comment to a suggestion she'd made about where to stop for lunch.

"I totally lost it," she said. "I was oblivious to our safety, to the kids in the back seat. I just couldn't snap out of it. Thank God Shane pulled over. It wasn't until I glimpsed the kids' terrified faces in the rearview mirror that I thought, 'What am I doing?'"

Shane also experienced explosive rages. Six months earlier, he'd punched the wall and broken a finger. He lifted his hand to show the scar on his knuckle. The trigger had been Elena planning a solo trip with a friend to decompress.

In *The Dance of Anger: A Woman's Guide to Changing the Patterns of Intimate Relationships*, women's psychology expert Harriet Lerner, PhD, talks about "countermoves" that occur in relationships when one member of a couple asserts a need in a new, direct way that the other partner finds threatening. With Elena and Shane, when one of them attempted to shift out of their enmeshed dynamic and gain greater autonomy, a countermove usually followed.

"I'm not sure anger's the problem, here," I said. "The problem seems to be *avoiding* anger. Anger's usually considered a secondary emotion because there tends to be a primary emotion under it, but it still offers us information and tries to guide us."

"But it's not like other emotions," Elena argued. "Anger's bad."

"Aggression and anger are different," Shane pointed out.

"Right," I agreed. "How we handle anger makes it destructive. It can result in aggression, but it can also connect you to yourself and other people. It depends on how you express it."

I shared with Elena and Shane what I knew about the work of Aaron Sell, PhD, an Australian social psychologist and assistant professor at the School of Criminology and Criminal Justice at Griffith University in Australia, who writes in the Theoretical Framework section of his webpage "anger is triggered when the mind detects that another person is not putting sufficient weight on the welfare of the angry individual." Sell's research shows how anger evolved to help us regulate conflicts of interest and make our own welfare more of a priority. Being aware of the evolutionary purpose of anger can help us understand how to use it productively and consciously before it morphs into aggression.

Elena had grown up with an explosive father who could be loving and generous but could also yell and rage, seemingly without warning. She described him as her very own childhood Dr. Jekyll and Mr. Hyde. Thanks to him, she'd become someone who tried to placate people—"freezing and pleasing"—and tried to avoid anger in any form.

By stark contrast, Shane's parents grew up in the era of Woodstock. They were vegan pacifists who believed that enlightened people only felt love. Neither of his parents had exhibited their anger directly, though he had often witnessed it seeping out in passive-aggressive actions and words.

Elena and Shane had seemingly opposite experiences of anger expression in their respective families, but both had evolved to view any outward expression of anger with fear and disdain. They'd been suppressing their anger because they thought this was the only alternative to indulging in it. But avoiding anger, and denying its function and purpose, creates new problems. Expressing anger in a healthy way starts with accepting it as an emotional experience we all have—often multiple times a day. Notice if you judge, deny, avoid, or minimize anger. Many cultures and societies, including in the United States, condition us to express or repress anger along gender lines. For many women, sadness is far more easily felt and accessed than anger. For men, the reverse is often the case.

Once you accept the emotional reality of anger, pay attention to the physiology of anger in your body. You may notice that fear or hurt usually precede it, though often this happens just outside of conscious awareness. The earlier you recognize your own anger signals, the sooner you can intervene and preempt aggression. Does your heart race? Do you grind your teeth? Is there a prickling sensation in your gut? Do you feel muscle tension around your eyes and forehead? Make a choice about how to proceed responsibly. Express your anger non-aggressively. "I'm noticing myself feeling angry. Please stop criticizing the way I'm driving, otherwise I'm going to pull over. I want to keep us safe." Or you might choose to distance yourself from the situation or person triggering you by taking a time-out. In "What to Do Mid-Fight" (page 138), I provide additional ideas for coping with anger.

If out-of-control anger or aggression continues damaging your relationship despite your attempts to create safety, it may be time to seek professional help.

Exercise

The Speaker talks about the ways anger was expressed—or not expressed—in their home growing up. Do you have any early memories of feeling anger? How did the adults in your life support you in expressing your anger? How did they respond to their own anger? What beliefs did you grow up with about anger expression? Have you ever had positive experiences with anger? Can you imagine noticing your anger in the future and telling your partner what you're feeling without blaming them? How might sharing your experience of anger without blame bring you closer?

Sample Exchange:

SPEAKER: In my family, anger and aggression were the same thing. The only person who was allowed to express anger was my father, and when he did, he was out of control and explosive. He would spank us or smack us. My mother got very anxious when my sister or I got upset or had a tantrum. She would panic. Any expression of anger seemed to overwhelm her.

As a girl, I learned that people with power got angry and used anger to dominate others and get their way, so I learned to do that, too. I never liked giving in and being dominated by my father or by anyone else. I think if I notice when I feel angry at you, I'll remember that love isn't about control and domination. I can just tell you I'm feeling angry and why.

LISTENER: I appreciate you letting me in on how you relate to anger, and for committing to a more conscious approach to expressing it with me.

29

Understanding Your Triggers

Elena and Shane took a radically new approach toward their experience of anger (see chapter 28). They stopped denying their anger and started noticing how frequently they felt it. They began talking to their elementary-school-aged children, Joseph and Rachel, about the importance of anger as an emotion.

"Mom and Dad are taking anger lessons," Shane overheard eight-year-old Joseph tell one of his friends after soccer practice one afternoon.

The most gratifying feedback on their progress with anger came from Joseph's counselor. During one of their treatment-plan meetings, she reported to Shane and Elena that their son seemed more relaxed and was getting into fewer fights at school.

The toxic waste of unprocessed anger that had been accumulating under the surface of their relationship was rising up, getting neutralized, and being safely disposed of.

One important step in this process involved identifying triggers.

An actual trigger is a device that releases a spring or a catch and sets off a series of mechanisms—a chain reaction of interlocking microevents. In the case of a gun, pulling the trigger causes it to fire. Just as with the trigger of a gun, psychological triggers cause things to fire rapidly through our limbic system. Virtually instantaneous emotional chain reactions typically occur outside of our conscious awareness and can cause us and others harm.

The concept of interoception—awareness of internal body states—originated in 1906 with Sir Charles S. Sherrington, a Nobel Laureate, who spoke about receptors in the body. Interoception is a skill that can support anger management. Mindfulness practices, such as meditation, expand interoceptive abilities. Therapy that focuses on tuning in to the body and moment-to-moment experiences can also increase awareness of sensations, thoughts, and emotional states. In his book *The Body Keeps the Score: Brain, Mind, and Body in the Healing of Trauma*, Bessel van der Kolk, MD, uses the term *interoception* to describe our ability to know what we feel and why, saying, "The greater that awareness, the greater our potential to control our lives [. . .] If we are aware of the constant changes in our inner and outer environment, we can mobilize to manage them."

In cognitive behavioral therapy (CBT), clients often keep a log of triggers, feelings, thoughts, and reactions. By bringing mindfulness to these triggers over time, your awareness grows and it becomes easier to *respond* rather than *react* as you move through triggering situations.

I had Shane and Elena each start a trigger log so they could identify patterns of when they were set off by each other's actions.

Shane identified Elena's disdainful facial expressions as a trigger for him, along with her contemptuous tone and her repetitive requests. When she asked him the same thing multiple times, he noticed feelings of shame and incompetence. His thoughts were, "I'm a terrible husband. I can't get it right." He responded by shutting down. This only fed Elena's frustration at having to repeat herself.

Elena identified her main trigger as Shane's excessive use of his cell phone and other digital devices. "When I see you on your phone, I want to scream," she said. Her reaction reflected her longing for intimacy in their marriage, but this trigger had roots in her personal history. Her parents had been avid TV watchers. There had been a television in every room of her house growing up, including the bathroom. She'd always felt like she was competing with TV shows and news programs for her parents' attention.

"Through the trigger logs, I've noticed that my automatic reaction when I'm angry is denial. I shut down," Shane said. "I had no idea I was so ashamed of my own anger. I automatically ignore it and force myself to act peaceful and calm."

"I'd much rather know you're angry," Elena said.

"What new response could you try out with Elena?" I asked. "Rather than ignoring or denying your anger or trying to act calm when you're not?"

"Tell her what I'm feeling?" Shane said. "It seems crazy to think something so simple could make a difference, or that I could actually do it, but I'm definitely going to begin seeing what happens when I do."

Elena and Shane spent 10 or 15 minutes a day between sessions noticing when they were angry, then backtracking and tuning in to the psychological, emotional, and behavioral layers of responses to the trigger. Talking about their discoveries taught them about themselves, their attitudes toward anger, and how they could relate to each other's emotions more consciously and empathetically.

Exercise

Both partners fill out a trigger log using a recent trigger. The Speaker then shares the trigger, their feelings, their automatic thoughts, or relationship horror stories (see chapter 4), and their reactive behaviors. The Speaker comes up with one new response they could try out in the same situation that might be self-compassionate and keep them connected to their partner.

Sample Exchange:

SPEAKER: I wrote about the trigger of your anxiety, specifically when I see you bite your nails. When I see that, I feel anxious myself. My automatic thoughts are, "She's not happy," and, "Something's wrong." Then my automatic reaction is to lecture you about how bad it is to bite your nails, how people at your job will notice you're an anxious person. One thing I could do instead is tell you, "I notice you're biting your nails and I'm wondering if you're feeling anxious. Can I take your hand or give you a hug?"

LISTENER: Thank you for sharing some of your triggers with me, and for allowing me a glimpse of the feelings, thoughts, and reactions that can go with them.

TRIGGER LOG

TRIGGER (who, what, where, when, how):

FEELINGS:
Bodily (sweating, shaking, etc.)   Emotional (sad, angry, helpless)

THOUGHTS ("I'm a failure," "Bad things always happen"):

REACTION (I criticize my partner, yell, withdraw):

NEW RESPONSE (I take a time-out, notice and label my feelings, breathe slowly):

stepping stone
WHAT TO DO MID-FIGHT

Romantic relationships are some of the most intense emotional attachments we create in our adult lives, and they make us feel all kinds of ways that don't make it into quaint quotations in Hallmark cards.

Even on your way to "no more fighting," you will have moments when you criticize each other, bicker and get irritable. Both of you, at different times, will be self-absorbed or show a lack of sensitivity. Realistic communication is imperfect. Falling short of our goals in the process of closing the gap between where we are and where we want to be is part of learning new skills. When fights happen, don't let them stop you from recalling to your overarching intention. Stay true to habits and practices that reduce unproductive conflicts and strengthen your bond.

I get this question a lot from couples: "We know how to try to prevent fights, and we know how to make up, but what do we do right smack in the white-hot center of a scary, hurtful argument?"

Here are 10 actions you can take mid-fight:

1. Recognize your relationship horror stories (see chapter 4).

2. Recognize you're in the middle of a fight. This can allow you to switch gears and know that something needs to be done differently and consciously *now*.

3. Bring your "true adult" into play (see chapter 17). Resist resorting to your "pseudo-adult strategies." Soothe your own "inner orphan."

4. Remind yourself you do have options even if things feel temporarily hopeless.

5. Practice "holding your relationship in high regard." This is one of five skills outlined by the founder of the Relational Life Institute Terry Real in his book *How Can I Get Through to You? Closing the Intimacy Gap Between Men and Women*. This means thinking positively about your relationship even when it feels anything but positive. Remind yourself that this moment is temporary and it doesn't define your relationship.

6. Use the Imago Dialogue with your partner, mirroring, validating, or empathizing. Take psychological ownership for some small part of what's happening between you.

7. If nothing you're doing helps, and your partner is still triggered, tell them you want to keep things emotionally safe between you by taking a brief time-out. You will come back in 15 or 20 minutes and try to address the issue when you feel more centered.

8. Do a re-do (these are explained in the next chapter). Restart the "scene" of your disconnection a moment or two before the trigger point and redo it more consciously and kindly.

9. Try a one-minute Vent Box (see page 55). Only use this mid-fight if your partner agrees and feels comfortable opening a Vent Box for you, and only if you can direct your frustration at the situation rather than at your partner. Venting at your partner mid-fight will only escalate it.

10. Use a Love Ritual on the spot, like a Feeling Check-in or an appreciation.

The Art of Repair

— Being *Right* or Being *in Relationship*
(Oliver & Gail)

— Remorse and Forgiveness
(Ayanna & Luis)

> The ego and the heart have different agendas for your relationship.

30

Being *Right* or Being *in* Relationship

Oliver and Gail came to see me soon after taking a two-week trip to Rome. Gail shied away from rules and loved surprises. Oliver valued predictability and responsibility. Gail had arranged their first vacation together overseas despite Oliver's trepidation. She'd studied art history in Florence and envisioned romantic dinners, museum tours, and late-night embraces on the steps of the Piazza di Spagna.

Oliver had never spent an extended amount of time in a place where he couldn't speak or understand the language. Having to rely on Gail as his interpreter was distasteful to him. He was overwhelmed by the new and different cultural cues. Gail interpreted his anxiety as judgment and a general lack of appreciation.

"Just admit what you did," Gail said. "That's all I want."

"You want me to take the blame," Oliver said, "when it was both of us."

"It was *not* both of us," Gail countered, as she pulled a notebook out of her purse and flipped through the pages. "You were stressed out on the flight and didn't want to hold my hand. You complained about everything. You refused to tour the Vatican. On June 14th—"

"Gail," I interrupted, "what do you need from Oliver in this moment?"

"Just to admit the truth," Gail said, closing the notebook in exasperation. "That's why I took notes. Because he can't admit when he's wrong."

Oliver shook his head.

Gail and Oliver's disagreements tended to devolve into a debate about right and wrong. My former couples supervisor and Imago Master Trainer Carol Kramer Slepian often uses the quote, "You can be *right* or you can be *in relationship*." This excellent maxim is a rescripting of self-help author Wayne Dyer's famous words, "When given the choice between being right and being kind, choose kind." There's a great deal of wisdom in both of these statements, especially for couples.

In her book *When Things Fall Apart*, American Tibetan Buddhist nun Pema Chödrön encourages people who are seeking more peace in their lives to resist the urge to "concretize"—to try to make someone or something bad or good in order to establish a false sense of security or control. When couples choose being in a relationship over being right, they're avoiding the temptation to concretize.

Once Gail understood that being right wasn't going to get her any closer to Oliver, she put away her notebook and dropped the evidence that proved her point. Although they couldn't necessarily go back to Italy to do things differently, Gail and Oliver did start practicing better communication skills (see chapters 3–7). After some initial skepticism, they even practiced "re-dos."

Re-dos are like another take of the same scene in a movie. They offer a second chance to approach a trigger point differently and de-escalate a situation by literally redoing the scene of your rupture. During your re-do, instead of saying, "Why don't you ever take walks with me?" you can ask your partner, "Would you like to go for a walk?" In turn, your partner can respond in a friendlier voice than they did during the first go-round. Instead of snapping, "Can't you see I'm working?" they might say, "Thanks for the invitation. I wish I could, but I'm busy right now."

Performing a re-do of a triggering moment, starting just before the trigger point and incorporating whatever your partner has told you they would need to feel more connected, can put things in perspective as you reenact the scene.

One day when Oliver picked her up, Gail felt upset that he didn't greet her. She could feel herself about to criticize him. Instead, she asked for a re-do. "Can we do this again?" she asked calmly. "When I approach, can you say, 'Hello, sweetie, good to see you,' look me in the eye, and give me a kiss?" Oliver recognized he'd been distracted and agreed to try it. Running through the scene again, he smiled, said, "Hi, sweetheart, good to see you!" kissed her on the cheek, and then they went on to have a pleasurable evening.

Even if re-dos lack spontaneity and seem performed, they can still effectively move partners toward repair, and sometimes bring humor and perspective to an overly weighty situation.

Giving up being right doesn't mean you give up your convictions. It means honoring a multiplicity of viewpoints. Rumi says, "Somewhere beyond right and wrong, there is a garden. I will meet you there." For couples, this garden is their relationship.

Exercise

Both partners take a few minutes to circle one thing they can't tolerate from the following "Convictions List," or come up with a conviction of their own. The Speaker shares their top conviction and why they feel so strongly about it. Then the Speaker reverses the conviction and imagines how the reverse might be true. How does it feel to do this? What would it feel like to give up the need to be right about this conviction in an argument with your partner?

Sample Exchange:

SPEAKER: The conviction I chose is, "Life is about having fun." I get nervous when relationships stop being fun and happy and get bogged down with heavy emotions and conversations. I've always struggled with this belief of mine that, "Life is about having fun," because as soon as you get emotional or serious, I feel like we're going down a path toward unhappiness.

The opposite of this belief would be, "Life is not about having fun," or, "Life is serious." So I can see how this might also be true. Life can be challenging, hard, and unpredictable. It makes me sad when I think that. Maybe that's why I want life to be all fun and no work. I don't like feeling sad.

LISTENER: Thank you for sharing one of your convictions with me, and for being willing to see that the opposite conviction can be just as true as the one you believe is right.

Convictions List

- Always assist others who are in need.
- Be polite no matter what.
- If you love me, you also love the things I love.
- It's important to be on time.
- Life is about having fun.
- Lying is unforgiveable.
- When you love someone, you make them feel important.
- It's not safe to relax and let go.
- In a close relationship, you share all your secrets.
- If you really love me, you'll remember what's important to me.
- You should take care of me when I'm sick.
- I have a right to go through your things since the affair.
- You should keep our problems completely private.
- If you're really generous, you offer to pay.
- It's essential to always celebrate anniversaries.

> Remorse sanctifies our imperfections; forgiveness unfetters our humanity.

31

Remorse and Forgiveness

Ayanna called me after Luis confessed he'd had a one-night stand with a hotel employee at a firefighters' annual conference.

"We're both devastated," Ayanna said. "We've been crying for days."

Luis was a lieutenant at a metropolitan firehouse, and Ayanna was a social worker. They'd been married for nearly eight years. Both Luis and Ayanna were hyper-responsible, took their jobs seriously, and were always going above and beyond what was expected at work. A few weeks prior to the incident at the firefighters' conference, Ayanna had found out she was pregnant. They'd both been surprised by the news, since Ayanna had been told by doctors for years that she would have trouble with fertility due to her endometriosis.

Luis had the physique and stature of a bodybuilder, but in our sessions, he sat hunched over, his shoulders collapsing over his broad chest. Despite his size, in his current emotional state, he seemed to take up less space in the room than his wife, who was slender, with short, close-cropped hair, and half his height in heels.

"I don't want this to affect the baby," Luis said. "I feel like a scumbag, like I've risked our family out of pure stupidity. I keep replaying what happened in my mind, trying to change it."

"I don't want you to torture yourself," Ayanna said sadly, offering him a tissue.

Luis shook his head and pressed his thumbs against his closed eyelids, reminding me in a way that was rather unsettling of the eye-gouging Oedipus at the end of Sophocles's play.

"I can't stand seeing the pain I've caused you," he said, in a tremulous voice.

Ayanna *was* in pain. She felt hurt and angry, but her own pain seemed to expand and multiply when she saw it reflected in Luis's face and distorted by his shame. As a therapist herself, she'd worked with couples struggling with betrayal and infidelity in her own clinical practice. Though she'd empathized with what they'd gone through, she'd felt certain that infidelity was not something she needed to fear in her own marriage, given Luis's character. Now, she felt naïve and foolish. She desperately wanted to forgive him, in part because she loved him deeply, but also because she knew feeling more relaxed and positive would be better for her baby.

"I want to move past this," she said. "I wish I could force myself to let go of my anger and resentment. I wish I could just forgive you and move on."

Forgiving your partner is more about opening to the possibility of forgiveness than actively making yourself forgive. When your partner is able to empathize with your pain and take responsibility for their part in causing it, a new—albeit delicate—bridge can span the gulf between you. When you're the partner who engaged in a hurtful behavior, taking ownership for your mistakes and experiencing and expressing your remorse can move you both through confusion and grief. Remorse lays the groundwork for forgiveness. It's easier to forgive someone when they fully grasp the impact of their poor choices.

Over time, Luis and Ayanna learned that prior to Luis's affair, they'd both prioritized other people's needs and neglected their own. This shared blind spot had left an intimacy vacuum. When Ayanna told Luis about her pregnancy, he'd felt overwhelmed but hadn't wanted to dampen her joy with his anxieties. What if he was a terrible father?

Ayanna worked on letting go of the old version of their marriage, one in which she had never doubted Luis and his commitment to her. As Buddhist teacher and author Jack Kornfield writes in *The Art of Forgiveness, Lovingkindness, and Peace*, "Forgiveness means giving up all hope of a better past." For Luis, the challenge was moving out of shame and risking greater emotional authenticity. Genuine remorse and forgiveness emerged in small moments—in feelings of gratitude and in cautious, restrained excitement about the approaching birth of their child. Ayanna started to see the importance of putting her own time together with Luis first—or at least on par with the time she spent serving others. Taking each other for granted was risky business.

Exercise

The Speaker talks about a situation in their life when they either felt remorse or forgiveness. What did you learn from this situation? What did it teach you about yourself? Were you able to express your remorse or forgiveness and have it received? If you weren't able to express it, how would you express your remorse or forgiveness now?

Sample Exchange:

SPEAKER: When I saw my father in the hospital after his stroke, I felt genuine forgiveness toward him for the ways he hurt me as a kid. His sadness was so palpable as he squeezed my hand. I could feel that he loved me. I don't think he meant to cause me as much harm as he did. If I could have voiced my forgiveness at that moment, I would have said, "I forgive you for being imperfect as a father and causing me harm as a result of your own pain and limitations."

LISTENER: Thank you for sharing this moment of forgiveness with me. I'm committed to showing up with both remorse and forgiveness in our relationship.

stepping stone
SENSATION IS
INFORMATION

We can develop and expand our ability to listen—and by extension, our ability to know and understand others—by spending time listening to ourselves. American philosopher Eugene T. Gendlin developed a practice called "Focusing," which involves clearing a mental space, connecting to a *felt sense*, finding a *handle*, resonating, asking and receiving (for more on this process see www.focusing.org/sixsteps.html). Many meditative practices also encourage deeply listening to ourselves. But contrary to popular opinion, listening to oneself like this isn't an esoteric practice. We all naturally do it. Self-attunement from a position of self-respect and self-appreciation is within our reach. No matter who we are or what we've done or failed to do in our lives, we're always worthy of our own attention.

Try closing your eyes and noticing what you feel in your body right now. Is there an achiness within you? A tightness in your chest? A feeling of heaviness around your eyeballs? See if you can identify the locations in your body and the sensations that are there and match them up. Play with matching different feeling words—like *vulnerable, lonely, sad, excited, angry*— to these different bodily locations and sensations. Over time you may begin to notice a subtle resonance when there's a match: a visceral "aha" moment. These moments often happen when your body feels "heard"— when the information it's carrying has been translated into self-knowledge.

Money Matters

— The Meaning of Money
  (Jordan & Barbara)

— My Money, Your Money, Our Money
  (Oliver & Gail)

Money is a
2.61-inch-wide and
6.14-inch-long screen
for our projections.

32

The Meaning
of Money

For Barbara and Jordan (see chapter 23), money was an invisible trip wire that kept popping up between them when they least expected it. They would be in the middle of something—taking a walk, finishing a meal—and seemingly out of the blue one of them would bristle at something that was said, react to a suggestion with suspicion, or withdraw in response to what they'd heard or misheard. Many of their mini-ruptures had to do with money.

"I don't know what happened," Barbara said. "We were paying the bill in the restaurant, and suddenly Jordan got this look on his face. I said, 'Are you okay?' and he nodded, but I could tell he was upset. I said, 'Should I contribute?' and he just gave me this nasty look."

"I just didn't need her money, that's all," Jordan said quietly. He extended his fingers and balled them into fists, suddenly observing the mechanics of his joints with a great deal of interest.

Money was linked to Jordan's sense of himself as a competent provider. When Barbara offered to pay, he felt inadequate and got reactive. But he also felt resentful, because he spent a lot of money on things they did together or consumed together—movies, trips, dinner, and groceries—and part of him wanted her to contribute.

The next week, Jordan expressed a desire to get clarity on a recent fight.

"We had a great weekend," he said, talking to Barbara. "We hung out on the roof, went dancing. We met up with friends for drinks. Then we got into some kind of a discussion about the pros and cons of having a kid, and I remember saying something you took the wrong way."

"You kept going on about how much a kid costs," Barbara said. "You were like, 'Did you know the average kid costs $250,000 for a middle-class family to raise, not counting college? We could buy a houseboat with that!'"

"Right," Jordan said, "I was trying to make conversation."

"We're talking about creating a life, here. About engaging in one of the most beautiful, miraculous acts available to us as human beings," Barbara began. "About growing a family together, and all you're focused on is money? I find that really sad."

Barbara seemed to be staring at the clock over Jordan's head.

These money trip-wire incidents were divisive and unsettling.

When Barbara had worked as a fashion model, she felt that the amount of money she'd earned had been a reflection of her value. Because her mother, who'd worked as a flight attendant and rarely spent time with her, had always given Barbara plenty of spending money, she'd grown up seeing money as a form of love. Barbara's ability to attract and accumulate money, desirable objects, and luxurious experiences had always seemed to offer her proof of her value, visibly to others but also less visibly to herself.

When Jordan worried about money or suggested there wasn't enough of it to do what they wanted—like have a child or go to Belize for a week—it cut to the core of Barbara's self-esteem. She interpreted his frugality as a devaluation of her.

For Jordan, money represented security. He'd been raised in a poor neighborhood in Philadelphia. He used to sleep buried under a pile of his own secondhand clothes because his parents couldn't heat their house. His standard dinner had been black beans from a can, applesauce, and carrots. His stepfather had seen him as a financial liability and criticized him relentlessly. Jordan had left home at 16 and started working in a restaurant. He'd always joked that he'd gone into the restaurant business because it was a surefire way of getting a hot meal.

Barbara and Jordan had assumed that money meant the same thing to each of them. It took time for them to understand what money represented in their lives as a result of the different forms of deprivation they'd experienced growing up.

Exercise

Take a moment to look at the following "Money Meanings List," and circle the qualities that resonate most for you. The Speaker then talks about the links between early deprivations, longings, and experiences with what money has come to mean for them.

Sample Exchange:

SPEAKER: My top three Money Meanings are Invulnerability, Security, and Power. We lived in a middle-class neighborhood but I almost wish we'd grown up in a neighborhood that reflected my father's true net worth more accurately. He was always in debt and always changing jobs, and my mom had her hands full with three kids.

I struggled with never being able to keep up with my peers who had cell phones and Nike sneakers and the latest gadgets. I got teased and bullied about being poor. Sometimes I couldn't even go on field trips, so I pretended to be sick. I mowed lawns and walked dogs so I could buy what other kids had. For me, money has always been a shield protecting me against ridicule. I feel protected when I wear name-brand sunglasses or a $2,000 Rolex, like no one can get at me, even though part of me knows it's BS. But because so much of my father's powerlessness stemmed from poverty, it's like I need to always prove I'm rich to feel strong.

LISTENER: Thank you for sharing some of your Money Meanings with me. I'm committed to talking more with you about money and how our different Money Meanings interact.

Money Meanings List

- Access
- Attractiveness
- Control
- Dignity
- Entertainment
- Freedom
- Greed
- Happiness
- Invulnerability
- Love
- Luxury
- Power
- Respect
- Safety
- Security
- Self-importance
- Self-worth
- Soullessness

> Beware of the cost—in resentment—of unclear money boundaries.

33

My Money, Your Money, Our Money

Despite their differences, money had never been a problem for Oliver and Gail (see chapter 30). When they moved in together, they divided up their separate finances clearly and took on financial responsibilities in a way that felt easy and equitable. Both Oliver and Gail—a freelance photographer—had been earning six-figure incomes, though Oliver, who worked as a CPA, had additional insurance and retirement benefits through his company.

When Oliver moved into Gail's rent-controlled West Village apartment, they continued to keep their money separate, though they opened a joint account for shared expenses, like food and household bills. They hadn't been in a rush to get married, but when Gail got pregnant, they decided to have a small civil ceremony at City Hall in lower Manhattan. After that, Oliver signed Gail up for coverage under his health insurance plan. Neither of them wanted to combine their money into a joint account. They enjoyed the sense of differentiation having separate accounts gave them.

"I know it's weird to say, but separating our money was sexier," Gail confessed. "I liked treating him to dinner, and I liked it when he bought me gifts. That money boundary gave us a degree of space and separation."

When their daughter Riley was born a few months later, Gail went on maternity leave and her income came to a screeching halt. Oliver began taking over payment of all of their household expenses, bills, and rent. They agreed this setup would be temporary.

"When are you going back to work?" Oliver would ask Gail occasionally.

"I don't know," Gail would say. "Nannies are expensive and so is daycare."

They began to fight more frequently. The smallest expense could trigger a conflict, with Oliver's resentment and Gail's defensiveness creating a mini-Molotov cocktail wherever they were, in a park, at a café, or on their way to visit relatives. Within a year, Oliver's resentment had them sleeping in separate beds. Although Gail knew avoiding work wasn't a solution, she justified her choice to turn down job offers by convincing herself that only she could take care of Riley. After arguments with Oliver, she got in the habit of cuddling up next to her sleeping daughter, soothing herself by staring at her angelic face. Motherhood had eclipsed both her marriage and her career.

"I didn't sign up for being the sole breadwinner," Oliver said when they returned to therapy. "I thought we were going to be equitable partners. Something's off-balance."

Gail knew she hadn't been completely up-front with Oliver about her professional insecurities, her low self-esteem, her feelings of attachment to Riley, and her fears of leaving her daughter in someone else's care. In one session, she admitted that part of her had grown so unhappy with who she was in their relationship that she sometimes wished Oliver would divorce her so she could live her life alone with Riley. It seemed like that would be easier.

Multiple challenges were wrapped up in Gail and Oliver's situation. They had to ask questions related to money, and whether or not it still made sense to keep it separate. How had the power balance shifted since Gail stopped working and earning her own income? What was the value of Gail's unpaid work? Should they open a joint account so Gail wouldn't be in the position of asking Oliver for help paying everyday expenses? Was it fair to expect Oliver to be the sole breadwinner when they'd had a different agreement before Gail got pregnant? What were the advantages and disadvantages of Gail seeking freelance photography work versus staying home? What would be the cost to their marriage if Gail didn't return to work and Oliver continued as the sole provider?

There are no absolute answers to these questions, just as there's no one-size-fits-all method or inherent advantage to either separating or sharing money within a couple.

For Gail and Oliver, asking the questions without anger or blame began reducing the tension that had built between them for over a year. Through therapy, Gail began to realize that her fear of letting someone else take care of Riley was actually a cover for other, deeper fears, which included fear of failure, fear of success, fear of taking full responsibility for her life, and fear of what she stood to both lose and gain if she opened herself up to the complexity of her often contradictory desires and lived her life more authentically and fully.

Within a few weeks of their first tough money discussions, Gail dusted off her lighting equipment and photography gear and drove to do her first photography gig since their daughter was born. Oliver spent the afternoon at the park with Riley, playing hide-and-seek and feeling more hopeful about his marriage.

Exercise

The Speaker talks about their money boundaries. Do you like having your own separate accounts, joint accounts, or a combination when it comes to sharing and separating finances? What are the pros and cons of having separate accounts? Of having joint accounts? What aspect of your money boundaries as a couple do you think could be clarified or improved?

Sample Exchange:

SPEAKER: I like that we have joint accounts for our money. I know I earn more than you, but it's a reflection of love and trust for me. One of the pros of our shared accounts is the ease of it. One of the cons is that sometimes the account drops and I don't know why, and that scares me. I wonder if there's been fraud on our account until you tell me how you spent the money.

One aspect of our money boundaries that I think we could improve is bringing more awareness to the money we spend. I'd like to talk for a half hour at the end of the week about any major upcoming expenditures, look at our credit card bills together, and just be more aware and transparent with each other about what we've been spending money on.

LISTENER: Thank you for talking about your money boundaries with me, for sharing what works for you, and for bringing up what you'd like to change.

stepping stone
TIME MANAGEMENT

In today's high-tech, busy world, focusing on the things that matter isn't easy. Many of us struggle to find time, or to use the time we have well, amidst a cacophony of cell phone pings and digital pop-ups, work-related emails, messages from friends and Facebook friends, and other far-too-accessible Internet distractions. When you factor in nonnegotiable commitments—kids' extracurricular activities, family members in crisis, the demands of evolving careers, and self-care—time can become an even more limited resource.

In his book *The Big Leap: Conquer Your Hidden Fear and Take Life to the Next Level*, psychologist Gay Hendricks talks about "Einstein Time." Einstein Time defies our traditional notion of linear time, which is "out there," scarce, and ticking away with every passing moment. Einstein Time, Hendricks says, comes from within. We're the source of this kind of time. When we take full ownership of our life, and begin to move through it as active agents rather than passive defenders, we generate the time we need to be where we need to be and do what we need to do. This is what we're aiming for within the Couples Time Container: Einstein Time, quality over quantity, depth over length. When you feel like there's "not enough time," breathe—slowly and consciously. Connect to the present moment. Appreciate what you have with your partner now and enjoy pursuing more together.

Your relationship has the potential to become a time generator. When you and your partner are connected, there's more energy, more aliveness, more motivation, more love, more joy, more *you*. The more of these things you have, the more you can expand time by enjoying time. Having time is the art of aligning where you are with where you want to be until the two are one and life has a timeless quality in each and every moment.

Coping with Stress

— Different Kinds of Stress
(Ayanna & Luis)

— Fight, Flight, or Freeze
(Brandy & Julissa)

Stress less,
love more.

34

Different Kinds of Stress

Ayanna and Luis (see chapter 31) had been running a stress marathon of sorts for several years, but in the last year—between Ayanna's unexpected pregnancy and Luis's one-night stand at a firefighters' conference—stress had turned into a crash course. Rebuilding trust in the midst of a pregnancy can be like patching a boat that needs to be repaired while it's still in the water.

Both Luis and Ayanna were anxious. Our sessions focused on identifying different kinds of stress and experimenting with helpful responses to it, individually and as a couple.

Most of us intuitively know that all stress isn't bad. There are actually two types of stress. Good stress—known as eustress—is a motivator. It improves our performance and feels exciting. It's short-term and manageable. The birth of a child, meeting a deadline, preparing for a wedding, moving to a new home, succeeding at something we've been working hard to achieve, going on a longed-for vacation—these "stressors" can all generate eustress. The other kind of stress, *distress*, is the type of stress most people mean when they say, "I'm stressed." Distress is negative and demoralizing. It decreases rather than enhances our ability to perform. Situations that commonly elicit negative stress are fights with our partner, the death of someone close to us, money concerns, getting fired, and illness.

With both eustress and distress, we're wired to react. Even when the situation isn't life-threatening, such as meeting an upcoming project deadline or getting a promotion, we may experience sudden or extreme change—even positive change—as threatening. Signals from our internal and external environments relay information at lightning speed to different parts of our brain, including the amygdala and the hypothalamus.

Our autonomic nervous system controls the physiological changes that power us up to cope with real or imagined threats. Once the threat has passed, it brings us back to homeostasis through a process known as allostasis. If we chronically experience either eustress or distress without a chance to power down and relax, key glands go into overdrive, releasing hormones like cortisol while reducing neurotransmitters like serotonin and dopamine. As a result, allostasis is harder to achieve. Too much cortisol can wreak havoc on the body. Chronic stress contributes to symptoms of anxiety and depression and raises the risk of high blood pressure, heart attacks, and strokes.

For cognitively oriented clients, Rational Emotive Behavior Therapy founder Albert Ellis's famous ABC Model can be used as a guideline for shifting distress to eustress. In the formula A + B = C, the first variable, A, is the activating event. The second variable, B, is the belief we hold about it, and C is the consequence. Distress, as the activating event, can be shifted into eustress, or the consequence, by front-loading Ellis' ABC equation with a new, more positive belief about our stressor.

"What's your good stress and what's your distress?" I asked Ayanna during one of our sessions. "Sometimes it helps to separate them."

"Looking forward to the baby's birth is good stress. The baby shower and my mother coming from Trinidad to stay with us for a few months is good. But then the same event causes me distress. I worry a lot. It's about trust, but not just trusting Luis. I find it hard to trust anything, right now, including my own body."

"And you, Luis," I asked, "are you aware of your different types of stress?"

"My good stress is looking forward to fatherhood," Luis said. "So many of the guys I work with are dads. They've been telling me stories. I'm excited, but I still wish there was more I could do."

Ayanna and Luis practiced what clinical professor of psychiatry and Executive Director of the Mindsight Institute Dan Siegel calls "Mindsight." Mindsight combines the concept of insight with mindfulness while also emphasizing interpersonal attunement. Practiced together, these things can gradually alter the structure of the mind to be less rigid and more resilient and flexible. Mindsight is the dynamic, interactive process of knowing your own mind while also knowing the mind of another. Ayanna and Luis slowed down and paid closer attention to the signs of their own and each other's eustress and distress. Through awareness and attunement, they used Mindsight to decrease their stress levels.

Greater attunement led Ayanna and Luis to make changes and take action. They signed up for a birthing class a couple of weeks prior to the baby's due date. They started experimenting with on-the-spot relaxation techniques, such as holding one another, counting their breaths, closing their eyes for five minutes as they imagined themselves in a beautiful place, touching foreheads while synching their breaths, and taking a break in the middle of a stressful activity to hold one another or go for a walk.

Exercise

Take two minutes to jot down the top five things stressing out your partner this week. Then compare lists. How accurate are they? How in touch are each of you with what the other is dealing with daily?

The Speaker then expands on what their partner got right and explains what they're dealing with that their partner wasn't aware of. The point of this activity is to remind yourselves and one another that you're both fighting your own individual battles and that you may not always be aware of what your partner is dealing with on any given day.

Sample Exchange:

SPEAKER: You got two out of five of my top stressors, wow! I'm surprised, since I haven't even told you directly about what's stressing me out this week. I'm also stressed about signing a lease for a new apartment, because I want to make the right choice and I'm afraid of getting ripped off. Having to go for a biopsy is very stressful. The other stressful thing I'm dealing with right now is the upcoming audit at work.

LISTENER: Thank you for sharing your top five stressors with me. It's good to know what causes you stress so I can be more supportive.

Partner's Top Five Stressors

1. _____

2. _____

3. _____

4. _____

5. _____

> Stress isn't meant to be chronic.

35

Fight, Flight, or Freeze

Brandy and Julissa were used to defying categories and overcoming obstacles. Brandy was a transgender woman of color, and Julissa was bisexual, the only child of Asian immigrants. One issue in their lives that weaved into all the others was chronic, low-grade stress.

"We both deal with stress poorly," Julissa said. "And we're stressed out way too much for our own good."

"Stress is stressing us out," Brandy said, in her rich Lauren Bacall voice. She leaned forward and took Julissa's delicate hands between her larger, manicured fingers. "We want to figure out ways to lower our stress levels together."

Many of the stressors Brandy and Julissa were dealing with were common, like paying bills, moving into a new apartment together, and pressures at work. But because both of these women had a long history of coping with varying degrees of traumatic stress from an early age in the form of emotional and verbal abuse and prejudice, minor stressors could have a major impact.

Brandy's primary stressors revolved around being respected at her job as a cosmetic consultant at Macy's, whereas Julissa's centered around her law firm, where she felt limited by the tedium of endless case study research work she was doing. She longed to be more involved in LGBTQ advocacy work.

"I want more authority and respect," Brandy said. "I'm good at making things happen. I don't just want to put makeup on people for the rest of my life. But when you're a person of color, and you're trans, managers look to find reasons to keep you down. That's stressful, every day."

Brandy and Julissa had both been born into a world that expected them to identify with their birth bodies, genders, cultures, and heterosexual-identity norms. Brandy had faced the poignant challenge of experiencing her true self trapped in a boy's body from her earliest years, an experience called "gender dysphoria." Even before she could speak, she'd rejected cars, trains, and other toys her parents bought her that typically appealed more to boys, and felt happiest when she was allowed to wear dresses and play with her sister's dolls. When Brandy had made suicidal gestures as a nine-year-old, her parents had finally spoken with a gender-identity specialist and started to accept her reality as more than just a "phase."

As mammals, we have three primary responses to stress: fight, flight, or freeze. The fight response to stress can give animals a brief hit of almost superhuman strength as they defend themselves. The flight response allows animals to feel danger in a split second and run. The freeze response is a last resort in seemingly hopeless situations. It can minimize pain in an attack and provide possible survival opportunities when there seem to be no options.

"I get stressed about going to the grocery store," Julissa noted, "or out to a restaurant. I'm wary of people, especially when I'm not dressed up in a suit."

"Would you describe yourself as a fighter, a fleer, or a freezer?" I asked.

"A freezer." Julissa shivered to make her point. She had learned to withdraw physically and emotionally when other kids teased her at school about her name, her body, or the shape of her eyes. "An ice-cold freezer. Sometimes a fleer."

In addition to our couples work, I gave Julissa a referral for a local therapist with experience in LGBTQ issues and trauma work. If you've experienced trauma by virtue of being socially or societally "othered"—dehumanized because of some quality, feature, or aspect of who you are—or if you've dealt with specific or repeated racial, sexual-identity, and/or cultural microaggressions, seeking community and professional support to create a countercultural experience of belonging and affirmation has the potential to become a revolutionary act of healing and self-love. You are worth it.

Brandy and Julissa began tuning in to their stress levels daily. They asked each other, "Stress level, one to ten?" If they weren't together, they called each other or sent a text. By monitoring their stress, they could reduce it. When one of them was at a five or above, they went into "stress triage," taking a time-out, listening to loving-kindness meditation audios or music, or replaying soothing, prerecorded statements they'd made for each other on their iPhones, like, "You're perfect the way you are," and, "You're completely loveable." Or they might take a bath, work out, or dance. If they were together, Brandy asked for what she needed—affection or reassurances. Julissa practiced "melting" her freeze response by tightening and relaxing all the muscles in her body several times and then letting Brandy hold her.

Exercise

Take two minutes to identify one recent stressful situation you experienced as a couple and write it down. Choose the number that best fits your stress level at its peak, with one being the lowest degree of stress you felt and ten being the highest. The Speaker then shares what they did in that situation. Did you fight, flee, or freeze? How did your stress reaction impact your partner? What are three stress triage options you could try next time in a similar situation to transition out of fight/flight/freeze and into connection?

Look at the Stress-response Styles questions that follow, and circle *T* for true or *F* for false. Based on your responses, is your tendency that of a fighter, a fleer, or a freezer? Do you engage in one, two, or all three of these stress reactions?

Return to the recent situation you identified earlier. Rate the stress-intensity level from one to ten. Then go through the listed response styles that follow, and select *true* or *false* to identify your default stress-response style. Is this a stress-response style you use frequently in other situations? If it is, how does it impact your partner? How might you respond differently in a stressful situation?

Situation: _____ _____ (Number ____)

FIGHTER

(T/F) I'm often on the lookout for judgment.
(T/F) I sometimes believe people are out to harm me in some way.
(T/F) I suspect people are looking to pinpoint my flaws.
(T/F) When people smile at me, I think they might be mocking me.
(T/F) I'm ready to defend myself in most situations.

FLEER

(T/F) My heart can beat really fast in awkward situations.
(T/F) I'd rather move away from a problem than confront it.
(T/F) Often when I get what I want, I feel scared rather than excited.
(T/F) I sometimes find people intimidating and prefer to get away from them.
(T/F) I tend to expect the worst and try to avoid new or unknown situations.

FREEZER

(T/F) I often feel helpless and like things can't be fixed.
(T/F) A lot of the time it's not appropriate or safe to express myself.
(T/F) Sometimes I feel nothing in stressful situations, just numb.
(T/F) I tend to believe nobody can help me.
(T/F) I often prefer to just lie low and let things pass.

Alternate Stress Response: _____

Sample Exchange:

SPEAKER: My stress response is to fight. A recent situation was when I was in the kitchen talking to my mother on the phone and you turned on the blender. I gave you a nasty look, made angry gestures, and finally put the phone on mute and yelled at you.

I imagine this fight response probably left you feeling disrespected, angry, and hurt.

I think a better response would have been to leave the room and finish my conversation elsewhere. I could have come back to you later when I was calm and let you know that when I'm on the phone like that and we're both in the kitchen, I need you to be patient and hold off until I'm done with my conversation before making noise.

LISTENER: Thank you for identifying your stress reaction in that situation and sharing it with me, and for recognizing a better way to handle situations like that in the future.

stepping stone
FROM DISTRESS TO EUSTRESS

Write one of your stressors related to doing this work in the space provided below. What do you believe about this stressor? What's the consequence to you, emotionally and psychologically, when you "add up" this stressor and your belief about it?

Using the same stressor, consider an alternative positive belief that is just as true as your stressful belief. Imagine how this new combination of A + B might shift C—the consequence—ever so slightly in the direction of being "good stress."

ACTIVATING EVENT ➡		BELIEF ➡		CONSEQUENCE
A	+	B	=	C
		Distress		
Missed our Couples Time	+	"We won't grow"	=	Fear, disconnection, tension, worry
		Eustress		
Missed our Couples Time	+	"I can be flexible and trust"	=	Connection, hope, motivation

Distress: _____

_____

Eustress: _____

_____

Parenting

— Parenting Styles
   (Randy & Felice)

— Blended Family
   (Will & Lani)

— In-Laws
   (Susan & Arjun)

36

Parenting Styles

After addressing some pressing issues in their marriage, Randy and Felice (see chapters 13 and 20) had the emotional stability they needed with one another to turn their attention toward their daughters and take stock of a few of their ongoing parenting challenges.

"My biggest concern with our parenting is the way we discipline," Felice said.

"Personally, I think you need to relax and let them be," Randy said. "I mean, they're kids. They're supposed to eat Doritos and watch YouTube."

"See, this is the problem," Felice said, turning to me. "He undermines me."

Felice had stopped working in order to raise their girls, with a part-time nanny, and she'd only begun taking on some part-time and volunteer work recently. Randy was around them less because of his work schedule, and although he intended to follow Felice's lead with limit setting and enforcing consequences when the girls didn't take care of their responsibilities, when the time to enforce limits came, he frequently contradicted Felice or let things slide. One complicating factor was that the girls seemed to require different amounts of discipline. Their daughter Olivia was much more prone to complete her homework regularly and set and clear the dinner table, whereas Charlotte put off homework and disappeared at chore time.

"They have different personalities," Randy said. "You're too hard on Charlotte."

"You're too *lenient* on Charlotte," Felice said. "She knows you'll let her off the hook no matter what she does."

Foster Cline, MD, and Jim Fay, cofounders of the Love and Logic Institute and authors of *Parenting with Love and Logic*, have outlined four common styles of parenting: drill sergeant parents, helicopter parents, laissez-faire parents, and consultant parents. Drill sergeant parents prioritize power and control, and expect children to follow rules and comply with demands or be punished. Helicopter parents, though well intentioned, try to rescue their children from virtually every uncomfortable experience, whether physical or emotional. They try to please their children, make few demands, and expect little. Laissez-faire parents give their children virtually no guidance, whether because they're detached, overwhelmed, or feel children learn best when they fend for themselves. Consultant parents set firm, thoughtful limits based on children's safety and the impact of their behavior on others. Consultant parents give children options within defined parameters so kids can think for themselves and learn from the results of their choices.

As drill sergeant parents, helicopter parents, or laissez-faire parents, we're usually either adopting our own early caregivers' parenting style or doing the opposite in an attempt to avoid hurting our children in the ways we were hurt. Spending time as a couple investigating your reflexive parenting habits, and working toward becoming consultant parents, can bring ease and flow to your interactions with your children and more peace to your home.

What Randy realized during these discussions about parenting styles was that with all the conflict and confrontation he navigated at work, he wanted to be a kid himself when he got home. He'd slipped into the habit of relating to his daughters as if they were friends. And while it's lovely to be friendly to our children, treating our kids as friends is more about our needs than theirs. As much as Olivia and Charlotte enjoyed their father indulging them in the moment, it was also unsettling to have so much power. More than getting their way, or winning power struggles, kids need to feel secure in their parents' authority, understand the reasoning behind limits, and have freedom to think for themselves and learn from their own choices.

Felice recognized that she tended to vacillate between the helicopter and drill sergeant parenting styles. Although this seemed in some ways to be an improvement over the neglect she'd grown up with, it was far from the conscious, grounded parenting she wanted to embody. Both Felice and Randy decided to contact a local parenting coach, and they scheduled a few online coaching sessions. It didn't take long to see links between their reactions to their daughters and what they'd experienced growing up. From there they found that it was easier to make adjustments than they had anticipated.

Exercise

The Speaker identifies the parenting style they most relate to: drill sergeant, helicopter, laissez-faire, or consultant. Try to be honest and nonjudgmental of yourselves and your partner. What was the parenting style your parents or primary caregivers used when you were growing up? What were the pros and cons of being parented in this way?

Do you find yourself shirking your inherent authority as a parent to minimize or avoid conflict, or going overboard in exerting your authority to control your children? Talk about one way your partner might be able to support you in being more of a consultant parent.

Sample Exchange:

SPEAKER: I know my style of parenting is mostly laissez-faire. I find myself so overwhelmed that I give up and withdraw. I don't want to be a drill sergeant, and when I see the way you are with the kids, it scares me. At the same time, I don't know how to contribute. So I let you take care of things and when things go poorly, I leave the room. I guess that's avoiding taking up my authority. In my family, my mother was laissez-faire. My father was a drill sergeant. I can see how I'm repeating that pattern with the kids, being laissez-faire like my mother.

I could be more of a consultant parent if we came up with a plan, set ground rules, and stuck to them. Like if we told the kids no screen time at the dinner table but they can read after dinner, and held them to their chores with reasonable consequences we both agree on and uphold.

LISTENER: Thank you for sharing your thoughts on your parenting style with me and how you think we could support each other in being more consultant parents.

> Biological families are given; blended families are earned.

37

Blended Family

Will and Lani had been married for a year. Will was a widower and Lani had been divorced for over a decade. Will's 12-year-old son, Maxwell, was refusing to do chores, come to dinner, or communicate with Lani. In addition, Will had found vape pens in Maxwell's backpack. When he confronted his son, Max said he hated his new family. He vaped to calm down and to defy his father. Kelly, Lani's 10-year-old daughter, was falling behind in school. She said she wanted to live full-time with her father, Lani's ex-husband.

"It's been really tough," Will confessed halfway through our initial session. He was a large man with thick, curly, gray hair. Everything about him seemed wise and expansive. "It's been harder than we thought. We've been arguing a lot and it's mostly about the kids."

Lani's eyes reddened and a tendon showed at the side of her neck. She struggled with the tissue dispenser momentarily and extracted more tissues than she'd bargained for.

"It's so disappointing," she said ruefully. "Coming together as a family has made things worse instead of better. Maxwell yells, slams doors, insults me. I yell back and feel like the evil stepmom, especially when Will doesn't defend me to his son. And Kelly refuses to help around the house, now, because she sees Maxwell playing video games all day long."

"Max is still grieving his mom," Will said, his chin pulsing for a moment as he struggled to contain his feelings. "He's going to a counselor but he's definitely having a hard time."

Blending families is rarely easy, and in this case, there was the added layer of a boy's grief as he mourned the loss of his mother. On top of that, Maxwell and Kelly had each other to deal with as stepsiblings. Kids can feel demoted in their parents' affections as they compete with a stranger for the limited resource of a biological parent's love.

Using listening, validation, and empathy techniques (see chapters 3–7), Lani and Will took time to hear and understand each other's fears and hopes for Maxwell and Kelly. They agreed to let go—for now—of their expectation of a seamlessly blended, happy family. Comparing their actual situation to an idealized version of family life was generating feelings of inadequacy and disappointment for both of them. Moving toward unity required a nuanced approach that included talking as a family about acceptable behaviors, creating time for family meetings where Maxwell and Kelly had a chance to weigh in on decisions and share their concerns and feelings, and establishing shared boundaries for both children.

We also discussed Dr. Stanley Greenspan's concept of "Floortime." Greenspan was a child psychiatrist who developed a powerful and effective intervention that came to be known as the "Greenspan Floortime Approach." Often, for parents, this means temporarily setting aside their agendas and literally getting down on the floor to follow their child's lead in imaginative play at their child's stage of development. Will and Lani knew it was good to spend time with Max and Kelly, but things had gotten busier in their lives and at work, which made prioritizing downtime with their children hard. It can also be easy to misread kids' oppositional behaviors as, "They don't really need me anymore." Greenspan describes Floortime as 30 minutes a day of active attunement to your child where they lead your interactions. Reading together or watching a movie are positive activities, but actual Floortime requires a parent's full attention on the child. It means you're fully focused and attuned, following and responding to your child's cues, and allowing them to direct the flow of the interactions between you for a limited period of time.

Will and Lani made a concerted effort to create Floortime with Max and Kelly away from all distractions, including one another. Will took up meditation and worked on staying centered and loving when Max complained, got angry, or behaved disrespectfully. He also made space in his own emotional world for his feelings related to his former wife's death.

Sometimes, Floortime with his son meant going to the local community center to play basketball. It could also happen during a bike ride or a trip to a skateboard park when Will put away his phone and stayed tuned in to Max, celebrating his skateboarding moves, responding to his comments, following his lead, and enjoying the nuances of his son's personality. Floortime also took place lying next to each other on the living room floor while Max talked about one of the video games he was getting really good at while Will listened, asking open-ended questions, or reflecting his son's pride and excitement in a connection he'd made with a friend.

It took only two weeks of Will's attentiveness for Maxwell's animosity toward Lani and Kelly to decrease. Lani, who was engaging in her own daily version of Floortime with Kelly, also noticed that her daughter seemed more positive about their new living situation.

Exercise

The Speaker talks about blending families. Do you feel aligned with your parenting styles? Do you feel supported as a parent or stepparent? Do the boundaries you set with all of your children, biological and nonbiological, feel appropriate? Identify an area you'd like to improve in your blended family and one way your partner can support you.

Sample Exchange:

SPEAKER: I'm afraid that we're living parallel lives in the same house—you with your children and me with mine. I've always known my kids harbored a secret hope that I'd get back together with their mother, and when you and I started dating and got married, it was rough experiencing their disappointment. I think I choose to do things separately with them because I'm conflict-avoidant and it just seems easier than trying to do things together with them and you.

I want all of us to regularly sit down to one family dinner, rather than eating a lot of little meals and snacks separately and at different times in the evenings.

LISTENER: Thank you for sharing some of your thoughts on our blended family situation and for asking me for what you think might connect us more.

In-laws are part of the package deal.

38

In-Laws

For many couples, the challenge of in-laws is uniquely frustrating. This had been the case for Arjun and Susan (see chapters 2 and 17). Although Susan's mother had passed away when she was a child, Bob, her father, was still involved in her life. Bob had done his best to accept Arjun as his son-in-law, but when he'd had too much to drink, his xenophobic views about Arjun's race and religion would leak through the cracks of his jokes and stories. At dinners with Bob, Arjun found himself pulled between angrily calling out his father-in-law and abruptly getting up and leaving the table.

"I can feel your dad's antipathy toward me," Arjun said. "I get the impression he's hoping we divorce so you can marry some right-wing Christian fundamentalist like him."

"Don't get mad at me," Susan said defensively. "I wish I could change him. I know he can be insensitive and say awful things, but it's really the alcohol." Susan felt equally pulled in two directions. On the one hand, she cringed every time her father's xenophobia surfaced. She wanted to tell him off for being closed-minded, selfish, and hurtful. But, on the other hand, she rationalized her passivity by holding on to the fear that anger wouldn't help the situation and might even make things worse.

And then there was Arjun's mother, who ignored Susan whenever they were in the same room, and communicated with her indirectly through Arjun. Although Susan had done her best to understand Indian cultural norms and the expectations and assumptions Arjun had grown up with, she was torn between her Western mind-set and Arjun's collectivism, where parents had more influence on their adult children's choices and decisions than Susan considered appropriate.

"The hardest thing for me about your parents is the way you defer to them," Susan said. "I hate how much power they have over you. I know you've gotten better at saying no, but . . ."

"It sounds like you're *both* struggling with family loyalties," I noted. "Creating a new family while being pulled by the strong undercurrent of your original family is disorienting."

When either Arjun or Susan set boundaries, their parents resisted them by shifting the blame onto their child's spouse and debating or disregarding their requests.

In 1968, Stephen Karpman, MD, wrote an article about what he called "the Drama Triangle." Karpman's theory suggested that people can find themselves circulating through three different roles in relationships that keep them locked in an unsettling and unproductive dynamic. These three roles—each located at one corner of a triangle—are the Persecutor, Rescuer, and Victim. In their dynamic with one another and with their parents: Arjun and Susan viewed their parents as the Victims, saw their partner as the Persecutor, and then they themselves took on the Rescuer role to keep their parents safe from their partner's judgments. This only succeeded in reshuffling Karpman's Drama Triangle with one another in different roles, where they soon viewed their in-law as the Persecutor, themselves as the Victim, and pressured their partner to be the Rescuer. It was a never-ending, diabolical merry-go-round.

Both Susan and Arjun felt responsible for their parents' emotions. They'd grown up with the implicit message that it was their responsibility to make sure their parents were okay and to create a bridge between their parents' problems and solutions. Susan had learned to cook when her mother died, prepared meals for herself and her father from the age of 10. She still went over to her father's house on Sundays to make and freeze his meals for the week. Arjun, who was born in the United States, had tutored kids in math at age 12 to contribute to household expenses. In high school, he'd won chess tournaments with cash prizes that paid for his parents' first car. By his third year of college, he'd been offered a six-figure job at a tech start-up, and although he didn't believe in what the company stood for, he'd accepted the job and worked there for a year to pay off his parents' mortgage.

Arjun and Susan began strengthening their loyalty to one another as a couple, and also to themselves. Moving into a more empowered, self-respecting dynamic meant communicating vulnerably about their feelings and needs when it came to interacting with members of each other's families. It also meant resisting the impulse to rescue their parents or succumb to the temptation to demonize their in-laws. Establishing boundaries that worked took grit, endurance, and compassion as their decision to step off the Drama Triangle merry-go-round was met with opposition and resistance. Gradually, as both sets of in-laws got used to the new rules of engagement, a healthier dynamic emerged.

Exercise

Take a moment to look at the Drama Triangle. Identify a situation you find yourself getting into regularly with one of your in-laws. Look at the roles of Persecutor, Victim, and Rescuer. In this situation, when your in-law responds to you in the way they typically do, what roles do each of you play? What role does your partner play or end up playing? In what way do you, your spouse, and your in-law cycle around the triangle?

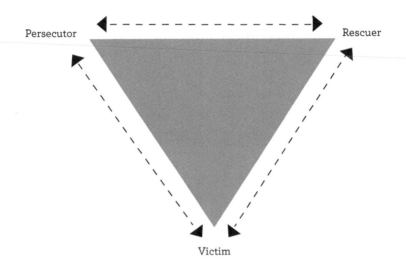

Persecutor

Rescuer

Victim

The Speaker then discusses how it feels to be in their "role" on the triangle and identifies one behavior they could practice to step out of this role. Remember to take full responsibility for yourself, your choices, and your emotions without laying blame. What's one thing your partner could do to support you in leaving this role?

Situation with in-law: _____

Instead of assuming the _____ role,
I could: _____

You could support me in exiting this role by: _____

Sample Exchange:

SPEAKER: My situation is when your mother comes over to watch the kids and she disagrees with how I do things. Whenever I feel like she's criticizing me, I assume the Victim role. I act cheerful and ignore her but I seethe with resentment underneath. One behavior I could take to step out of this role is to respond to her directly. I could say, "Nana, I know you were a really good mom. You raised an amazing son. I'm not perfect as a mom, but it hurts when you tell me I'm not doing things correctly just because you and I have different parenting philosophies. I'd appreciate it if you would focus on what I do right." One thing you could do as my partner is just hear me out when I'm upset about your mom. Just say something like, "Yeah, she can be tough."

LISTENER: Thank you for sharing more about the role you take on with my mom when she visits. I see your willingness to assume responsibility for yourself in this situation and change the dynamic with her. I'm so grateful for that.

stepping stone
MOVE IT

It's impossible to feel without moving. Our chests rise and fall more rapidly when we're excited, the foot at the end of our crossed leg jiggles when we're anxious or restless, our throats tighten and our eyes blink back tears when we're taken off guard by our sadness or gratitude. Muscles expand or relax in response to undercurrents of emotion. Whether we're aware of it or not, we're constantly being moved by feelings.

When it comes to processing emotions, movement doesn't always get the airplay of the more "respectable" cognitive forms of healing work, at least in Western culture. But movement is an essential gateway to our emotions. The more our emotions are able to surface freely and pass through us, held within our conscious awareness, the more we can integrate them into who we are and benefit from the wisdom they contain.

Expressive movement isn't a way of life reserved for performance artists. It's available to anyone interested in knowing and fully experiencing their inner reality. You can find your own ways of expanding your emotional access through yoga, running, dance, jumping up and down, rolling around on the floor, engaging in high-energy sports with your partner, or taking long walks in nature.

Maybe there's fear or grief within you that needs the vibration of your vocal chords to fully emerge, or joy that's aching for the breadth of your arms to reach outward through your fingertips, or sadness that longs to contract your body into a ball for the tears to release and flow. Pay attention to the tug of your emotions and how they're trying to move you out of the angles, lines, and boxy compartments of "acceptable," socially sanctioned movements, gestures, and behaviors.

Femme! is a class geared toward people who identify as female and want to explore expressive movement. These classes are one way of tasting the power in consciously moving emotions through your body and allowing them fuller expression than what is typically available to us in our day-to-day lives. This type of embodied movement was developed by inspirational speaker and somatic healer Bernadette Pleasant as a way for women to safely unleash the emotional intelligence that's already present in their bodies.

Love Languages

— Identifying Your Love Language
(Caleb & Viola)

— Speaking Your Partner's Love Language
(Caleb & Viola)

— To-Do Love Lists
(Caleb & Viola)

39

Identifying Your Love Language

Caleb and Viola were in their late fifties and had been married and living together for five years. They were both widowers who had met at a bereavement workshop. Their own children were grown and were starting families. They'd called me "just to give therapy a try."

"Should we really invest a lot of money and energy trying to change at this point?" Caleb asked. "Or do we just accept things the way they are? That's the million-dollar question."

"What would you like to change?" I asked.

"I wish Viola would recognize everything I do for her," Caleb said. "I take care of a lot of stuff around the house and behind the scenes. It may not be all that romantic, but it's important. Like getting our HVAC fixed. And I wish she'd save her money and stop buying me presents. It's like she thinks every day's Christmas. I've never been big on Christmas or presents."

"I try not to compare Caleb to my deceased husband, but I'm used to being with someone who values my thoughtfulness," Viola said. "The reason I don't focus on what he does is because I could care less about all that practical stuff. He does that for himself, not me. When we're both dead, the HVAC system and the fact we got our taxes in on time won't matter in the least."

In his book *The Five Love Languages*, Gary Chapman, PhD, explains how Love Languages are one way of thinking about how you give and receive love. I've found this framework extremely useful in couples work. When it comes to understanding how to love another person, many of us try to love others as *we* want to be loved, not as *they* need to be loved. This means that while we think we are showing them how much we love them, the actions we are taking don't have the same meaning to them as those actions do to us. By exploring your own and your partner's Love Languages, you can love each other with greater confidence and less misunderstanding.

The Five Love Languages are Acts of Service, Receiving Gifts, Quality Time, Physical Touch, and Words of Affirmation. There's no hierarchy in these Love Languages: They're all equally valid and equally meaningful to the receiver, particularly if it's their way of experiencing love.

For someone whose Love Language is Quality Time, a partner's attention and full presence feels deeply fulfilling, affirming, and loving.

When Physical Touch is your Love Language, warm physical contact, hands-on touch, embraces, and loving caresses melt your heart. Through touch, magic happens: You're home. Sexual intimacy tends to be a major aspect of this Love Language.

For people who experience love through Words of Affirmation, love hits the mark when your partner verbalizes it, using language that's specific, meaningful, and validating.

If your Love Language is Acts of Service, it's when your partner goes out of their way to *do* something for you that you feel most loved. Submitting the insurance claim, picking up your dry cleaning, or arranging a birthday party for your child can all show your partner's intention to make your life easier or more pleasurable through action-oriented love.

When Receiving Gifts is your Love Language, you feel loved when your partner gives you a meaningful gift at the right moment in a way that demonstrates how well they know you. It isn't about materialism. Gifts demonstrate—in a visible, visceral way—your partner's attunement to who you are and what you value.

Caleb identified with Acts of Service and Physical Touch as his Love Languages, whereas Viola found herself identifying mostly with Quality Time and Receiving Gifts. They had been giving each other love in the ways they themselves wanted to receive it, rather than tailoring the love they gave to their partner's preferences. By identifying their Love Languages, Caleb and Viola got clarity on why the love they expressed seemed to miss the mark despite their good intentions, and what form their love would need to assume to really, truly take root in their partner's heart.

Exercise

Identify your primary Love Language. To learn more about each type, I highly recommend reading Gary Chapman's book, referenced previously. When identifying your Love Language, don't overthink it or worry about "getting it right." Go with your gut. The Speaker then talks briefly about how, where, when, and from whom they received this type of love growing up. If they didn't receive it—or didn't receive enough of it—the Speaker shares what it felt like to long for this love.

Sample Exchange:

SPEAKER: My primary Love Language is Words of Affirmation. People never really praised me when I was growing up. I've read about how you're not supposed to praise kids because it makes them depend too much on praise, but I could have used more specific praise, more words that expressed the good people saw in me. I felt the absence of Words of Affirmation, especially because my twin sister got it all the time, from my mother, my father, teachers, and relatives.

LISTENER: Thank you for sharing and exploring your Love Language with me. It's empowering to know more about what I can say and do to show you I love you.

40

Speaking Your Partner's Love Language

Once Caleb and Viola (see chapter 39) had identified their Love Languages, their low-grade dissatisfaction started making more sense. It wasn't that they didn't love and respect each other, or even that there was a personality mismatch. The crux of the issue lay in the ways they expressed and received love. Unless Caleb's love took a form that Viola could authentically receive and metabolize, it didn't register.

"Now I know why you don't really care when I do things for you," Caleb said. "I speak to you in Acts of Service, and you speak Quality Time and Receiving Gifts."

"When you gave me that birthday card last year, I was so happy," Viola said. "You took the time to think about me and write from your heart. For me, that was a dream gift."

Caleb laughed and shrugged.

"I'm simpler than you. Hold my hand and make me a cup of coffee and I'm happy."

"All this time I was giving you gifts," Viola said, "and begging you to go for walks when your Love Languages are Physical Touch and Acts of Service."

I shared a personal story with Caleb and Viola that illustrates a painful truth about love. I'm not a plant person, but I do have a ponytail palm that's been with me since I started working as a couples therapist. One day I noticed its leaves were turning brown at the ends. I gave it more water than usual, sure this would perk it up. The leaves drooped. So I gave it more. And more.

Finally, after a few weeks, I picked it up and carried it down the hall to the bathroom. My goal was to drench it in water. I hoped this would finally save it and turn its yellowing leaves jungle green again. But when I lifted the base of the plant from the pot over the sink, what I saw shocked me.

The pot was full of stagnant water. The roots looked waterlogged. They were nestled in a porous container that had been designed to keep them dry. I'd been drowning the plant with what I thought it needed. In fact, I hadn't understood what it needed.

This can happen to a couple when you stubbornly give the kind of love you assume is good for your partner rather than being curious about the love your partner actually needs to receive.

Viola gave Caleb gifts, and when he seemed dissatisfied, she gave more gifts, which distressed Caleb more. When Caleb saw Viola looking sad or dejected, he did things for her—speaking in Acts of Service. But Viola's primary Love Language was Quality Time. By doing things for her, Caleb got busier and gave her less Quality Time than she'd been getting before, which only increased her loneliness.

After our conversation, Caleb and Viola began looking for opportunities in their everyday lives to show each other love in the ways that were most meaningful to the other person. Viola reminded herself to touch Caleb whenever she passed him in a room, even if it was only a gentle brush of his shoulder.

Caleb made an effort to initiate moments of genuine connection. "Do you want to sit on the porch for a few minutes?" he would ask. Or, sometimes, "How about we go get a coffee in town?"

Like a ponytail palm, relationships are resilient. They can recover when you take time to pay attention to them, notice what enlivens them, and find the right ways of nourishing them.

Exercise

The Speaker talks about their partner's Love Languages. What are some of the insights you've had? What do you think will be easy or challenging for you about showing love through your partner's Love Language, in the ways they want it most? Share one action you could engage in on a more regular basis that seems aligned with your partner's primary Love Language.

Sample Exchange:

SPEAKER: It's helpful for me to know that your main Love Language is Physical Touch and that Physical Touch relates to your desire for sex. Now I get why you're always so eager to be sexual. Maybe that's why you always say you feel more loving toward me after we engage sexually.

I don't think it will be easy for me to show you love through touch, since I avoid it and need a lot of space. Touch makes me antsy. At the same time, I think I can begin to touch you more throughout the day in certain, small ways. One thing I can do is take your hand, put my hand on your arm, and maybe ask if you'd like a shoulder massage when you look anxious.

LISTENER: Thank you for sharing your thoughts about my Love Language and for considering some new ways you can give me love that align with my needs.

41

To-Do Love Lists

Caleb and Viola (see chapters 39 and 40) were ready to take the guess-work out of giving and receiving love. Drawing from Gary Chapman's Love Languages framework, they'd identified the love "delivery systems" that worked best for them and gained more insight into which Love Language resonated most for their partner.

Caleb had been "speaking" to Viola in Acts of Service and some-times Physical Touch rather than in her Love Languages of Quality Time and Receiving Gifts; Viola had been speaking Receiving Gifts and Quality Time to Caleb when the love he needed was Acts of Service and Physical Touch.

"It all makes sense," Viola said, "but I'm still having a hard time translating these concepts and insights into actual behaviors. Because his languages aren't mine, I can't always come up with ideas or think of how to show love in ways he'll feel and receive."

"I can sometimes think of ways to have Quality Time together," Caleb said. "But I've never been a good gift-giver. With gifts, I really don't know where to start."

"Get me some flowers," Viola said. "Pay attention when we visit flea markets. Yesterday, at that street fair we went to, remember how I stopped at certain display tables and pointed at things I liked?"

Viola and Caleb had spent over two-and-a-half decades expressing love in ways that had felt comfortable and familiar to them without even questioning how their love was being received. In their previous marriages, they'd never had the luxury of making their own needs a priority. They'd been frustrated a lot and learned to accept what their spouses offered while focusing on raising their children.

They both wanted more from this marriage, and without children to distract them from each other the stakes felt higher.

It's going to feel unnatural to invest time and thought into loving your partner in new ways. Just like with an actual language, until you start to immerse yourself in the language you're studying, and you begin to speak it yourself, it's all in your head. When it comes to expressing love, it's about practicing new behaviors.

As an Imago therapist, I learned to help clients put together lists of caring behaviors they felt showed affection. These lists are made in part by recalling specific actions and words partners once effortlessly gave during the courtship phase of their relationship. The lists I help partners write once they understand one another's Love Languages include these behaviors, while specifically homing in on the Love Language aspect. I call them "To-Do Love Lists" (TDLs, for short). Whether they're used as guides, mnemonic devices, or motivators, TDLs help couples translate love into action.

Caleb and Viola each took five minutes to write down several doable, precise actions rooted in their Love Languages that their partner could take to show them love. They committed to expanding their TDLs whenever they got new ideas, and to talking about how it felt to be on the receiving end of them. While creating and using these lists can feel like it removes spontaneity from the process, I encourage clients to see TDLs as training wheels preparing you to be more spontaneous with these types of behaviors down the road.

Caleb's TDLs:

- Hug me in bed before you start going about your day.
- Initiate any kind of sex with me that would give you pleasure twice a week.
- Offer to set up one of my medical appointments when I procrastinate.
- When I'm out in the garden weeding, come outside and offer to help.
- When you walk past me in the house, touch my back or squeeze my arm.

Viola's TDLs:

- Buy me flowers and place them on the table with a love note.
- If you see me sitting alone, pull up a chair and join me without an agenda.
- Sit next to me in the evening when I'm watching the news.
- Take my hand, ask me how I'm feeling, and listen to my response.
- When we're eating a meal together, leave your phone in another room.

Exercise

Briefly write out your "To-Do Love List." Bring to mind your primary and secondary Love Language and identify five actions, stated clearly and succinctly, that would delight and please you if your partner took them. The Speaker then shares how it might feel to experience their partner engaging in these actions. When each partner has shared, exchange TDLs and commit to doing at least one of the actions on your partner's list every day.

Sample Exchange:

SPEAKER: For my "To-Do Love List," I chose the following behaviors: 1) Buy me a small gift, 2) give me a two-minute long shoulder massage, 3) pick me up from the subway station after work, 4) help me clear the table after dinner, 5) plan a special night out for us once a month. These behaviors resonate with my Love Languages of Receiving Gifts and Acts of Service. If you did one of these a day—or even every couples of days—I would feel special, loved, and appreciated.

LISTENER: Thank you for creating and sharing your TDLs with me and for giving me this opportunity to show you love in a way that syncs with your Love Languages.

Your TDL

1. _____

2. _____

3. _____

4. _____

5. _____

stepping stone
IT'S ALREADY HAPPENING

Growing together isn't something that will take place later: It's happening now, no matter where you are in this process. Even when the outcome appears to be radically different from what you're aiming for, that doesn't mean you're not growing. You're still present in your life with a degree of openness and curiosity, learning what works and what doesn't, expanding your interoception skills, and developing Mindsight (see chapters 29 and 34). By showing up willing to connect with yourself and your partner in your Couples Spot, you're doing the work. Too often, we're raised to acknowledge our accomplishments only when they're grand, noticeable to everyone around us, or aligned with a preconceived notion of what victory looks like. But all major successes result from the many humbler, less obvious achievements that preceded them.

Take time to notice, acknowledge, and enjoy your successes with your partner, big or small. Give yourselves credit for your willingness to explore and adjust course again and again. Just as a ship's destination can alter by a thousand miles with the slightest turn of a rudder or tick of a steering wheel somewhere along its journey, couples can also change where their relationship takes them by making small course corrections along the way.

Sexuality

— Desire Discrepancy
(Will & Lani)

— Understanding Sexual Shame
(Will & Lani)

— Erotic Blueprints
(Gail & Oliver)

42

Desire Discrepancy

When Lani and Will got married, their primary focus was on blending their two families (see chapter 37). Will had lost his wife to cancer two years prior to meeting Lani, who had been divorced for over a decade. Although living together had initially been difficult for Will's son, Maxwell, and Lani's daughter, Kelly, within six months their kids were getting used to each other and their new stepparents, and home life felt much more stable and harmonious.

"Since things are getting better with the kids," Lani said, stealing a quick glance at Will, "maybe we can talk about some of *our* own personal challenges now."

It looked as though a powerful industrial fan had just been turned on and pressed Will against the back of his chair. He gripped the armrests and his chin drew back.

"Sex isn't an easy topic for us," Lani said by way of explanation.

"We thought it was hormonal." Will raised one of his hands and rubbed his temple. "My doctor ran tests, checked my testosterone levels. There's nothing wrong with me physically."

Talking honestly and directly about sex and desire isn't easy in any context, and doing it in front of someone else, including a therapist, can feel awkward and uncomfortable. It's important to do it anyway. Most of us grew up unable to ask sexuality-related questions freely, research sexuality openly with encouragement and education, or learn, safely, through trial and error, without an overdose of shame and judgment, how to be our full, complex, puzzling and fascinating, ebbing-and-flowing erotic selves.

"The doctor offered me Viagra. I hate the idea of getting hooked on a pill for a hard-on," Will said. "It's pathetic. Is this what I've come to?"

"We have other kinds of sex," Lani said as an aside, "but I really crave intercourse. I think Viagra is something we could try if you'd stop judging it as some kind of horrible nail-in-the-coffin of your sexuality. It might get us over the hump."

"Over the hump?" Will asked, his tone playful.

Lani's face brightened and we all laughed.

Therapists sometimes refer to the difference in desire levels between members of a couple as "desire discrepancy." Over the course of a long-term partnership, desire levels can flip, with the lower-desire partner feeling more desire, and the desirous partner feeling less. Many elements influence desire levels: body image, unprocessed trauma, hormonal changes, illness, lack of safety, power dynamics, social conditioning, stress, too little closeness, too much closeness, and confusion about the interplay of masculine and feminine energies are all common factors.

In her Erotic Blueprint Breakthrough Course, sexologist and author Jaiya outlines different sexual states—Adventurous, Asexual, Curious, Healing, Resting, and Transformational. When one partner is in the Curious, Adventurous, or Transformational state, it can be challenging to sexually engage with a partner who finds themselves in the Resting, Healing, or Asexual state. Whatever the cause of desire discrepancy, for both partners, it can hurt.

Educator and activist Emily Nagoski, PhD, deconstructs the emotional, cultural, and biological intricacies of desire in her book *Come as You Are: The Surprising New Science That Will Transform Your Sex Life*. She talks about two systems that govern our desire: the Sexual Excitation System, or SES, and the Sexual Inhibition System, or SIS. The SES responds to whatever it interprets as "sexually relevant stimuli" received through the senses or thoughts. These stimuli aren't absolute and vary from person to person. Remembering the kids are with their grandmother, listening to sexy music, and the smell of your partner's skin all have the potential to activate your SES, if these things are interpreted as sexually relevant to you. The SIS is the system that's sensitized to threats and "puts the breaks" on your arousal. Threats can range from fearing a partner's judgment in bed to the possibility of contracting an STD or of an unwanted pregnancy. The more the SIS is activated, the less *willing* a person is to participate in the process of becoming aroused.

According to Dr. Nagoski, learning how to "turn off the offs" of our Sexual Inhibition System is a critical part of enhancing our arousal, perhaps more even than "turning on the ons."

Talking about their different desire levels helped normalize what Lani and Will were going through and reduce their fears of sexual disconnection. They also began looking at the beliefs they'd grown up with that had shaped their current sexual fears and longings.

Will brought more awareness to the ways he could reduce his SIS by allowing Lani to scratch his back every night after the kids were asleep and giving himself permission to take Viagra without making it an indictment of his sexual prowess. He also increased his SES by engaging in low-stakes, sensual, pleasurable activities with Lani, such as listening to music, dancing together, kissing without an agenda, and having a shower together before going to bed.

Exercise

Take a moment to read the following two lists, and circle possible ways to experiment with turning off your Sexual Inhibition System and turning on your Sexual Excitation System.

The Speaker then shares an erotic date-night scenario they'd like to commit to in the next week, along with three ways to turn off their SIS and turn on their SES.

Erotic Date-night Idea: _____

_____

_____

_____

_____

Sample Exchange:

SPEAKER: The scenario I came up with is you and I going out on a hiking trip for the day and then spending the night in that beautiful log cabin we went to last year overlooking Lake George. To turn off my SIS, I'd need to prepare ahead of time, remember food, gear, bug repellant, and blankets. I'd need to leave work behind so I could focus completely on us.

To turn on my SES, I could send you sexy texts for a couple of days in advance of our trip, and hopefully receive texts back from you. I could get enough sleep, lift weights, and exercise the day before we leave, and maybe go for a run to clear my head. I could also make sure I bring a lamp and my portable phone battery so we can have music.

LISTENER: Thank you for sharing your erotic date-night idea with me, and for sharing what you could do to minimize your inhibitions and maximize your excitement.

Turning off Sexual Inhibitory System (SIS)

- Fully discuss and put to rest my fears of STDs.
- Fully discuss and understand our views of pregnancy and the choices we're making (if relevant).
- Clear my head of work-related responsibilities.
- Create a regular time/space to connect physically and sensually.
- Take care of hygiene-related issues that create self-consciousness during sex.
- Stop multitasking.
- Minimize the possibility of interruptions.
- _____
- _____
- _____

Turning on Sexual Excitation System (SES)

- Kiss for a few minutes.
- Put on music I like.
- Talk about sexual fantasies for a couple of days in a row.
- Put on clothing that appeals to my senses.
- Read erotica.
- Take a walk and enjoy nature, the breeze, the smells, and the sights.
- Work out during the day.
- _____
- _____
- _____

43

Understanding Sexual Shame

Will and Lani (see chapters 37 and 42) took their sex life seriously. Though Will had initially refused to take Viagra, he agreed to try it as a way of reducing his performance-related anxieties and getting out of his sexual rut. A combination of factors—from unprocessed grief about his deceased first wife to self-consciousness—seemed to be getting in the way of his sexual bond with Lani.

Although Lani and Will were older and had both had a variety of sexual experiences with a number of past sexual partners, being in a committed intimate relationship can unearth layers of conditioning and shame that brief romances or passionate love affairs never quite reach.

"I've always felt wrong sexually," Lani said, a shift in her voice hinting at the hidden reservoir of emotion she carried related to this topic. "Like I'm a hypersexual freak."

"I think it's great how sexual you are," Will said.

"Thank you," Lani said. "But I still feel like my sexuality turns you off."

Lani remembered having always felt desirous, despite the fact that in her Italian immigrant family, her Catholic schools, and her predominantly white, middle-class community, intergenerational, cultural, and societal messages she'd received had repeatedly shamed her sexual-desire levels. She'd learned early on that lust in a woman was dangerous or evil, or both.

Will's shame was related to being a man who preferred taking a more submissive role, though he enjoyed holding leadership and authority positions in other areas of his life. His well-intentioned mother had raised him to believe that men's sexuality, unchecked, was violent and aggressive, something that had to be restrained and monitored. As it turned out, Will's desires, once he felt comfortable enough to share them, involved power dynamics, clothing fetishes, and role-playing. He'd felt judged for his erotic preferences and tastes early on in his life and internalized these judgments. It had been easier in his prior marriage to simply go numb, go through the motions, and shut down his true sexuality.

All of us pick up on messages that shape our views of sex from the moment we're born, long before we have any idea what sexuality is. We very quickly learn whether or not it's good and pleasurable to live inside of our bodies. We discover whether we can express the full range of our emotions or whether it's best to keep feelings in check. Our pleasures and joys are met with varying degrees of approval and disapproval, and from that, we stifle certain preferences while allowing others free rein. We pick up on whether it's okay to be physical and sensual through hearing, sensing, smelling, tasting, touching, through our fantasies, creativity and imagination. We note whether the world meets us with approval when we express ourselves in a fully embodied, physical way, and whether the boundaries we set are respected or transgressed.

Messages are constantly being transmitted to us as we grow up, shaping our sense of ourselves as erotic beings, whether through others' expectations and demands; social media and the arts; the way adults model love, touch, affection, and sexuality; the gender-segregation of clothes, books, and toys in stores; and the hidden gender hierarchies and unspoken rules related to physicality and sensuality in classrooms, on playgrounds, and in our own homes.

Will and Lani took a deep dive into sexual shame, supporting one another in the process. Will recognized that when he felt ashamed of some aspect of his sexuality—real or imagined—he numbed himself and shut down. Sometimes he lashed out, judging Lani as "insatiable" or "too much." This fed into her self-condemnation and confirmed her worst fears about being "a freak." She'd always feared her sexual appetite made her unlovable. Her strategy for avoiding shame, though not particularly healthy or successful, was to blame herself and deny her needs.

Lani and Will practiced a "huddle" mentality (see page 79) by creating a running log of "Shaming Commandments." These were negative messages that impacted their sexuality, many of which they'd received growing up. Both in and outside of our sessions, they examined each commandment they identified along with associated memories. Then, they created a new Sex-Positive Commandment they could consider adopting in its place.

Exercise

Take two minutes to look at the following "Shaming Command-ments" and "Sex-Positive Commandments," or to write your own in the spaces provided. Circle the ones you can relate to. The Speaker then identifies one Sex-Positive Commandment they could begin to adopt in place of an old, Shaming Commandment.

Sample Exchange:

SPEAKER: The Sex-Positive Commandment I would like to adopt is, "Thou shalt enjoy your senses fully, loudly, without restraint; you're not responsible for other people's responses or reactions to you." This would replace the Shaming Commandment: "Thou shalt contain and tone down your enjoyment while eating, drinking, playing, touching, singing, dancing, etc., because showing too much pleasure and vitality attracts attention." This Shaming Commandment has made it hard for me to enjoy my body fully.

LISTENER: Thank you for sharing your Shaming Commandments with me, and for being willing to adopt Sex-Positive Commandments so we can have more fun sexually.

OLD, SHAMING COMMANDMENTS	NEW, SEX-POSITIVE COMMANDMENTS
Thou shalt not be naked; it makes you a target.	Thou shalt find safe places to be naked.
Thou shalt not enjoy your body too much.	Thou shalt enjoy your body to the max.
Thou shalt not attract too much attention.	Thou shalt take in all the attention you want.
Thou shalt contain and tone down enjoyment.	Thou shalt eat, drink, play, and enjoy fully.
Thou shalt not touch your own body too much.	Thou shalt touch your body generously
Thou shalt not brag or receive compliments.	Thou shalt unapologetically receive.
Thou shalt not touch other people.	Thou shalt touch consenting others.
Thou shalt not take risks.	Thou shalt risk full aliveness.
Thou shalt not go too far from home.	Thou shalt explore and learn.
Thou shalt stay small to protect yourself.	Thou shalt expand to experience life fully.
Thou shalt not be messy.	Thou shalt be messy as f*ck.
Thou shalt refrain from losing control.	Thou shalt find times to surrender control.

> Erotic Blueprints
> are maps to the treasure
> of pleasure.

44
Erotic Blueprints

Gail and Oliver (see chapters 30 and 33) were sexually frustrated.

In the beginning, sex had just happened, as is the case with many couples. It had been uncomplicated. Gail had wanted it; Oliver had wanted it. No matter what else was going on in their lives, sex had been a delicious, reliable pleasure they could both count on.

But over the past few months, Gail wasn't as responsive to Oliver. She mentioned body aches, picked fights, or made abrupt decisions in the middle of an evolving sexual interaction, offering Oliver no options other than to halt his initiatives and withdraw to his side of the bed, his body buzzing unpleasantly and his mind in turmoil.

"I tell you what I want and you don't do it," Gail said, her voice rising plaintively.

"Yeah, right," Oliver said defensively. "No matter what I do, it's wrong."

"I'm really asking for too much?" The high-pitched trill to Gail's voice made her sound decades younger than she was. "I don't like limp touches, weak kisses. Just grab me!"

"Sorry, I'm not going to pin you down and push you against the wall *Fifty Shades of Grey* style," Oliver said, frowning and crossing his arms over his chest. "That's not me."

Sexologist and author Jaiya has created a sex-positive framework of Five Erotic Blueprints for understanding sexuality and sexual preferences: Energetic, Sensual, Sexual, Kinky, and Shapeshifter. Each Blueprint has a positive side, a shadow side, and specific needs. Exploring and making sense of these Blueprints, and how they relate to you and your preferences, can support a more fulfilling and less inhibited erotic flow with your partner. This tends to be a better alternative to binary thinking, particularly about sexuality: good and bad, normal and abnormal, right and wrong. Binary thinking polarizes couples and leads to cold sheets and untested bedsprings.

The Energetic Erotic Blueprint describes highly sensitive individuals who are often orgasmic and sometimes hypersensitive and judgmental ("My sexual way is better than yours"). Energetics may see sex as "more than just physical." Approached too quickly or too directly, they can short-circuit, and they can also dissociate in bed if they get caught up in pleasing their partner at the expense of their own erotic needs. Energetics often require light touch, eye contact, breathing, and lots of space for arousal.

The Sensual Erotic Blueprint describes individuals who prioritize aesthetics, beauty, and the importance of sensuality lived through their senses. People with this Blueprint can get easily distracted by something in their internal or external environments during erotic encounters and can find themselves chasing elusive orgasms. Sensuals need peace of mind, a clear shift between "ordinary life" and a sexual encounter, and intense, varied sense experiences.

The Sexual Erotic Blueprint points to individuals who love sex in its purest, most direct form: nakedness, genitals, orgasms, penetration. In this Blueprint, rapidly ignited, spontaneous desire is the norm. The goal can become much more of the focus than the process, and sex without orgasm can feel distressing or disappointing. Sexuals need plenty of genital attention, orgasms, oral sex, intercourse, sexual predictability, frequency, and often visual erotic stimulation.

The Kinky Erotic Blueprint describes sexually creative, adventurous individuals who enjoy drawing erotic pleasure from pushing edges and boundaries and defying taboos. Without caring relationships that make room for them to explore and accept their sexuality, individuals with this Blueprint may struggle with inhibiting shame. In *Becoming a Kink Aware Therapist*, coauthors Caroline Shahbaz and Peter Chirinos emphasize the need for people with atypical sexualities, such as BDSM, to find affirmation and acceptance in communities of like-minded individuals. People who identify with the Kinky Blueprint need support and freedom to explore as well as education on engaging in edge-pushing erotic play safely.

People who identify with the Shapeshifter Blueprint are more or less equal parts of all four of the other Erotic Blueprints. They are sexually sophisticated and versatile lovers. They can get bored easily, be overly flexible in meeting other's needs, and lose their own desires in their chameleon-like sexuality. Shapeshifters need change, flexibility, and variety.

For Oliver and Gail, approaching their sexual issues as collaborators rather than antagonists was a game changer. Erotic Blueprints offered a bridge across their apparent sexual incompatibility. Gail discovered that her main Blueprint was Kinky whereas Oliver's was Sexual. Seeing their sexual needs through the lens of Erotic Blueprints helped make sense of why they craved different activities, stimuli, and types of touch. Their struggles had nothing to do with an inability to desire one another. Oliver's fears of sexual failure shifted as he got more curious about Gail's Blueprint type.

Exercise

Take two minutes to identify your Erotic Blueprint. You may feel a resonance with more than one—that's normal. Which one seems to fit you best? Be willing to "try on" different types or go to the website www.eroticbreakthrough.com prior to meeting in your Couples Spot and take the Erotic Blueprint quiz.

The Speaker talks about their Erotic Blueprint. Why do you think this Blueprint captures, or partially captures, your sexuality? If you could ask your partner to fulfill one of your Erotic Blueprint needs, what would it be? Light touch? Intense sensation? More sex? Exploring taboos safely and consensually? Consensual psychological games or role plays? Can you ask for one specific thing you'd like to receive from your partner sexually?

Sample Exchange:

SPEAKER: The Erotic Blueprint I most resonate with is Energetic, although I feel like I also relate to the Sensual Blueprint. What I identified with was the need for light touch and space. I always seem to get most turned on when you're on the other side of the room, just looking at me, or when you're at work and you flirt with me by sending me random, sexy texts.

I need a slower process to get turned on. Next time we're being sexual, you could keep your distance from me for five minutes and come closer little by little rather than all at once.

LISTENER: Thank you for identifying and sharing more with me about your Erotic Blueprint and your needs. Knowing more about who you truly are erotically feels exciting.

stepping stone
WHAT'S IN A WORD?

Sex. For a little word, it's pretty loaded.

The World Health Organization defines sexuality as "a central aspect of being human throughout life [that] encompasses sex, gender identities and roles, sexual orientation, eroticism, pleasure, intimacy, and reproduction. Sexuality is lived and expressed in thoughts, fantasies, desires, beliefs, attitudes, values, behaviors, practices, roles, and relationships. While sexuality can include all of these dimensions, not all of them are always felt or expressed. Sexuality is influenced by the interaction of biological, psychological, social, economic, political, cultural, ethical, legal, historical, religious, and spiritual factors."

What are the limiting definitions of sexuality you're ready to shed?

Our own sexual aliveness can be linked to positive and negative events in the past. These encounters remain deeply encoded in our bodies. Even if we haven't cognitively grasped how our history affects who we are today, or how we respond to our partners in the present, the residual effects of old traumas resurface in our reactivity, defensiveness, avoidance, and inhibitions. If there's been a history of neglect, abuse, or boundary violations in your life, sexuality and desire can remain stubbornly contradictory and confusing. As the tidal wave of #MeToo sexual-harassment revelations shows, now more than ever, people remain confused about their own and each other's sexuality. This has painful consequences in committed relationships.

Try saying the word *sex*. Say it several times. What do you notice? Do you find the word enlivening or awkward? How does it feel? Is it soft and gentle? Harsh? Clinical? Raw? Sexy? Uncomfortable? Maybe you notice a jumble of mental pictures, or internal resistance in the form of a tightening sensation in your chest or gut. Or maybe nothing at all happens. Noticing what the word evokes for you is a simple way of gathering data and acknowledging your sexual truth.

Jot down your associations, both for the word and the concept of sexuality. Don't try to make what you write sound different, better, more proper, or more objective: write freely. Give yourself full permission to be honest, open, and emotional.

Relationship Wreckers

— Addictions
  (Brett & Joyce)

— Dishonesty
  (Elly & Sebastian)

— Wanting What We Don't Have
  (Brandy & Julissa)

45

Addictions

Brett and Joyce had been living together for two years. They had
a one-year-old son, Colin. When they came to see me, Joyce had
stopped breastfeeding so she could transition back onto a low dose
of Prozac, which her primary-care doctor had prescribed for her anxiety symptoms. She'd been worrying a lot more since Brett took a job
bartending at a hotel.

"The pay is good, and there's not a lot of other work out there
right now," Brett said. "I don't drink that much, really. Only when
a customer buys me a beer. It's part of the job."

"I have a bad feeling about it." Joyce shook her head.

When Joyce met Brett, his driver's license had been suspended
after two DWIs and he was doing community service at the hospital
where she worked as a nurse. They started to date on the condition
that he stay away from bars and bartending, go to AA meetings,
and find contracting work. He was an electrician by trade. But then

Colin was born, her disability payments ended, and they'd been hard-pressed for money.

"I don't agree with everything in AA," Brett said. "It's not a disease for everyone. I'm not getting hooked. Believe me, I'm not my father."

"Can you understand Joyce's concern?" I asked. "After the two DWIs?"

"Those happened after my dad died. I was in a dark place," Brett said. "I'm better."

"Having a kid has made me hypersensitive," Joyce said. Her voice was trembling. "I don't want either of us to repeat the patterns in our families. And it can happen so easily."

Brett's eyes reddened. He leaned forward and placed one hand on Joyce's leg.

"Hey," he said. "We're not repeating any patterns, okay?"

The American Society of Addiction Medicine (ASAM) defines addiction as "a primary, chronic disease of brain reward, motivation, memory and related circuitry." Although addressing and working through addiction is beyond the scope of this book, there are very few couples who haven't felt the chill of addiction in some form or sensed the shadow it casts across their hopes for a happy future. Alcohol and other mind-altering substances, video games, social media, online shopping, recreational and prescription drugs, pornography, traditional and electronic cigarettes, soda, junk food, every imaginable type and style of coffee—instant pleasures fill our lives at every twist and turn, offering to stimulate us or distract us from our boredom, numbness, or emotional pain, available more quickly and easily than ever before in the age of the World Wide Web.

Nothing is inherently wrong or bad about pick-me-ups or jolts of pleasure; it's how we use or abuse an activity or a substance that turns it from something that can temporarily give us a lift or a thrill into a potentially damaging compulsion.

In *The Big Disconnect: Protecting Childhood and Family Relationships in the Digital Age*, Catherine Steiner-Adair, EdD, explores how even our devices have become an addiction of sorts, the pings and dings and clickbait giving us intermittent dopamine hits and neurochemical highs.

Brett and Joyce began to face the reality of addiction in their lives. They had both grown up in families where their parents' addictions had been hidden and minimized. Joyce had grown up in Arizona, the daughter of a Native American and a German immigrant. Both her parents had been drinkers, but her mother was also a gambler. Her mother's gambling habit left Joyce's family in financial ruin. Brett's father, a retired Vietnam veteran, had suffered from PTSD. When he drank, he'd been physically and verbally abusive to both Brett and his mother.

Joyce had a good reason to fear that Brett's past issues with alcohol, and his current access to alcohol, were a dangerous combination. Carlo DiClemente, PhD, in *Addiction and Change: How Addictions Develop and Addicted People Recover*, discusses the stages of addiction recovery: Precontemplation, Contemplation, Preparation, Action, and Recovery Maintenance. Over several sessions, Joyce decided she would live with her brother until Brett changed jobs. Brett recognized the seriousness of the threat to his family if he continued to bartend and drink. He moved from the Contemplation phase of change to Preparation and Action, giving notice at work and beginning to attend AA meetings.

Brett and Joyce's struggles with addiction weren't over. One thing was for sure: Ignoring the problem was an ineffective solution.

Exercise

The Speaker discusses the role addiction has played in their life. What were the addictions you were aware of in your family of origin? Was there a substance or a behavior—whether food, alcohol, shopping, TV watching, or prescription medications—people turned to when they were unhappy? How did addiction impact you? How did your own addictions affect you? What have you done to cope with them? Is there something in your life that you crave or overuse, now?

Sample Exchange:

SPEAKER: My family was addicted to food. They used it as a form of emotional anesthesia. We were all very overweight as a result. It affected every aspect of our lives. My father basically ate himself to death, sitting on the couch watching TV, clogging his arteries. My mother cooked for us constantly. I think it was the only way she could show us how much she loved us. I used to take all kinds of things to my room: cookies, candies, junk food. That was how I soothed myself. I buried my emotions in a perpetual sugar rush.

I was ashamed of the way I ate, ashamed of my body. Kids teased me. But I didn't know how to eat differently, or how to soothe myself in any way other than by eating sweets. Since then, I've learned how to eat well and junk food no longer rules my life, but I still crave sugar, especially when I'm sad. Sometimes with you, instead of letting you know how I'm feeling, I eat.

LISTENER: Thank you for letting me in on your history with addiction. I want to support you in talking to me rather than falling back on food.

46

Dishonesty

Elly contacted me to "work through a crisis" with her boyfriend, Sebastian.

Elly was in her mid-fifties, a warm, attractive, and confident woman who had spent most of her life in the Foreign Service. Since retiring, she'd taken a part-time job at a pharmaceutical company. Sebastian was 15 years younger and worked as a corporate head-hunter. Elly had recently discovered he'd been accruing major debt on his credit card for the last 10 months and lying about it. He now owed creditors close to twenty thousand dollars.

At the start of our session, when I guided Elly and Sebastian to center themselves and check in with their intentions for our work, they seemed calm, though I noticed one of Sebastian's eyes twitch, and Elly was rubbing her thumb against her index finger. Sebastian—tall and well-built—looked like he might have been brought to life from the cover of a bodice-ripper novel. But the whites of his eyes looked watery and bloodshot when he faced me.

"My intention is to understand you. I don't get how you've been lying to my face," Elly said quietly.

Sebastian took a breath, gathered himself, and shook his head.

"Why couldn't you say, 'Hey, I'm strapped for money'?"

"I don't know," Sebastian said, looking down.

"Can you put words to what you're feeling?" I invited Sebastian. When he seemed at a loss to respond, I offered him choices. "Guilt? Inadequacy? Fear?"

"All those," he mumbled. "I didn't realize how much I was spending."

"Really?" Elly asked. "You didn't realize you were buying boxes of hundred-dollar cigars?"

"Okay, I did," Sebastian said quietly. "I lied. I guess I lie a lot."

There was a long, awkward silence.

"How is that to tell the truth about lying?" I asked. It may have sounded like a stretch to focus on this, but in accelerated experiential dynamic psychotherapy, tracking and highlighting what are called "glimmers"—the small, easily overlooked signs of the transformative potential that's already there in a client—is a guiding principle. This was a glimmer worth exploring.

Sebastian took a breath. His body relaxed.

"It feels good," he said. "It's a relief. Because it's the truth. I do lie. A lot."

"I'd really like to know what else you've been lying about," Elly said, crossing her arms over her chest.

Sebastian had never really allowed himself to take in the reality of how much his lies hurt people. Lying had been a form of self-protection that had become habitual. He'd grown up lying to minimize feelings of inadequacy, guilt, and shame. As a child, his mother had suffered from a debilitating disease and he'd lived with her in the dirtiest, smallest house on the block. Being honest as a kid had felt unsafe, like he was setting himself up for pity and ridicule.

We talked about the impact of Sebastian's dishonesty on Elly, who did her best to resist judging him. This wasn't easy. She felt angry and hurt. Whenever she was scared he was lying to her again, she wondered aloud if he was a narcissist. She expressed her sadness and disappointment and tried to understand the chaotic emotional puzzle of his lies and half-truths. She also took ownership of her own issues, admitting the ways she had enabled Sebastian's lies, and some of the ways she lied, too: mostly to herself.

Dishonesty is a part of our everyday realities, whether we admit to it or not. We all lie, though usually without malice. We respond, "I'm fine," to a greeting when we've just spent an hour sobbing into a pillow. We gush over a gift we'll never use. We say there's traffic rather than admitting we're running late because we didn't leave on time. Interestingly, in her book *Liespotting: Proven Techniques to Detect Deception*, certified fraud examiner Pamela Meyer presents data showing that on average, people lie less often to their spouses than to other people. Honesty is vitally important to sustained and prolonged intimacy. Call it radical honesty, courageous vulnerability, authenticity, or transparency—as long as we're not in a coercive or abusive relationship, choosing to be honest rather than deceptive can make us stronger individually and as a couple.

The more we're able to be ourselves in spite of our fears, the more approval we're showing for all aspects of who we are. If our partners know what's good for them, they learn to appreciate the less-than-perfect parts of us that we honestly share, since this gives them permission to accept their own underbelly, and to be more of who they are with us.

Exercise

The Speaker chooses to share a "white" lie they've told recently. Remember, as the Listener, your job is to make it safe for your partner to share, to refrain from judging, and to honor the courage it takes for your partner to be honest. As the Speaker, the lie can be something to do with your appearance or your age. Maybe it's something related to a skill you believe you lack, such as making money, driving a car, or swimming. The Speaker talks about what it would take to approach this aspect of themselves with acceptance and honesty.

Sample Exchange:

SPEAKER: I haven't always been honest with you about the exact number of beers I drink when I go out with my friends. I'm often afraid you'll use it against me the next time I tell you I'm going out. I lie because I find it uncomfortable when you criticize my drinking or try to control it. To approach this with more self-compassion, I would need to accept the fact that I may upset you or disappoint you, or that you might get angry because I don't see things the same way you do.

If you heard me out without judging me, I might also be able to hear you. Maybe we can find a way to deal with this more honestly if we address our different anxieties.

LISTENER: Thank you for being honest with me. It takes courage to share this. I appreciate you considering talking about this situation more honestly.

47

Wanting What We Don't Have

Brandy and Julissa (see chapter 35) had decreased the amount of stress they felt in their lives and jobs by tuning in to their bodies and bringing their stress levels down a few notches consistently every day through a variety of mindfulness and body-based techniques. Brandy had been more visibly relaxed in our sessions. She'd been promoted to a managerial position at Macy's, which had been a point of pride for her. Julissa had been putting together a pro-bono workshop for queer women in abusive relationships, teaching them their legal rights.

But one afternoon, when Julissa and Brandy came into my office, they appeared somber.

"I'm just going to say it," Brandy said. "You're pulling away. I can tell."

Julissa stiffened and turned away, as if Brandy had suddenly pulled open the curtain of her dressing room without warning her in advance.

"You're right," Julissa said coldly. "I have been."

"I want to feel connected," Brandy said, nervously adjusting the floral headband that kept her amber hair out of her immaculately made-up face. "I'm not trying to crowd you. I know you need space."

"Look, it's Kane," Julissa said ominously, then shook her head and went silent. Kane was her ex-boyfriend. More than once, Brandy had expressed her fear that Julissa would decide it was too hard to be with a transgender woman and go back to dating her ex.

Perspiration glistened on Brandy's brow.

"He's been texting me." Julissa's words ran together as though she was afraid that if she didn't say them all at once, she'd never get them out. "I miss feeling normal. I feel awful saying it, or even wanting it. I just want to feel like a regular person sometimes."

Fantasizing about an ex-boyfriend or ex-girlfriend, wondering whether they can give you more of something you need than your current partner can—normalcy, in Julissa's case—isn't unusual. Social exchange theorists see it as the underlying relational calculus that informs whether or not we choose to stay with someone.

Whether it's a long-term marriage, a friendship, or just a two-hour-long conversation with a fellow commuter on a train, social exchange theory is based on the premise that we see our connections, either consciously or unconsciously, as dynamic interplays of shifting rewards and costs. As long as the rewards we get are higher than the costs, social theorists believe, we'll stay. Many factors can impact the satisfaction we receive from the rewards of committed relationships, including our perception of what's available to us elsewhere in the form of "outside options." When Julissa compared being with Brandy to being with Kane, the "cost" of being with Brandy seemed to outweigh the benefits in this moment.

Social theorists call this process "Comparison Level for Alternatives," and although it's a natural human tendency, and can serve us in many social exchanges, particularly in relationships that become unfair or imbalanced, it can also crack the foundation of a good connection.

I guided Brandy through the Imago Dialogue process (see page 32). Rather than focusing on her defensive reactions, I reminded Brandy that what Julissa was sharing wasn't about her. Brandy mirrored Julissa's thoughts, fears, and longings, validated why Julissa would want the experience of "normalcy" she'd felt with Kane—a straight, white man—in a world that targeted LGBT individuals and women of color. There were risks in being partnered with Brandy and moving through the world as a queer/trans couple. Prejudice and hate-crime statistics are tragically real.

"I have to admit that Kane would never have been able to do what you just did," Julissa said when Brandy had finished empathizing with her. "I think I forget important things like that. You let me be me, and, honestly, I'm grateful to you."

By admitting how wanting what she didn't have distanced her from Brandy, Julissa cleared an emotional space to take in what she did have: emotional safety that came not from being camouflaged, or passing as something she wasn't, but from being loved for who she was.

Exercise

Take two minutes to look at the following list and circle, or write in the spaces provided, three things you view as the most significant benefits of being in a relationship with your partner. The Speaker then shares why these things are important to them.

Sample Exchange:

SPEAKER: The three biggest benefits I get from our relationship are being understood, being supported in my dreams, and the way we laugh together. With you, I feel safe and grounded, because I know you get me, the way I see things and how I feel. It's important for me to feel supported in my dreams because I was always told by my ex-girlfriend that my dreams were "unrealistic."

LISTENER: Thank you for sharing how our relationship benefits you and why it's important.

Benefits

- I can count on you.
- We have fun together.
- You help me take care of myself.
- We have great sex.
- You're always there for me when I need you.
- You contribute financially to our household.
- You contribute your time, efforts, and energy to maintaining our household.
- You divvy up household duties with me fairly.
- You get my sense of humor and laugh with me.
- We have great travel adventures together.
- Your companionship keeps me connected.
- You put effort into creating a beautiful home for us.
- You support my goals and dreams.
- We're a great team socially.
- You understand me.
- You're an amazing father/mother to our child/children.
- _____
- _____

stepping stone
RADICAL HONESTY SHARES

There are many ways we bend the truth. Sometimes, communicating our feelings, experiences, or actions to portray ourselves in a more favorable light is a protective reflex. Being honest takes mindfulness. Taking liberties with the truth seems to be a part of how we're wired, and may even be an undervalued form of self-care, depending on the context. We may slant things to make ourselves look more charitable, productive, kind, or responsible. We may change a detail or alter a fact, exaggerate a reaction or a response, not because we're calculating and deceptive, but because we're social creatures with goals, fears, and desires in our interpersonal exchanges.

Radical Honesty Shares can be a powerful tool for coming into alignment with the truth. Like Love Rituals (see chapters 13–15), Radical Honesty Shares can be turned into a daily habit that increases emotional safety. Valuing the parts of yourself you're tempted to hide, letting your partner see your blind spots, errors and character flaws, signals to them that they can also show up with the parts of themselves they'd rather pretend didn't exist. Radical Honesty Shares, practiced with an eye to reducing judgment, can increase self-approval as well as your partner's approval of themselves. They can foster more forgiving and accepting norms within your relationship.

Here's a personal story:

A few months ago, I went to get coffee in my husband's convertible on a beautiful, sunny summer morning. He frequently encourages me to drive his beloved car whenever I feel like it, and occasionally he has also gently reminded me to remember to put the top up.

After my drive, I returned home and began answering emails.

By the time I closed my computer, it had been raining for several hours.

The top was still down on the convertible, just as I'd absentmindedly left it, and the car was drenched. There was a layer of water three inches deep on the floor mats. Opening the doors produced mini-waterfalls that splashed across the rain-dimpled driveway. With some effort, I got the top up, though the automatic windows had stopped working. I covered them with trash bags.

This situation called for a Radical Honesty Share. My gut clenched at the thought of it. But to bend the truth in situations like these reinforces our own belief that we can't be loved and accepted as we are. It cheats our partners of the opportunity to have their feelings and reactions.

"I made a mistake," I told my husband, when I finally got up the nerve to call him. "I left the top down on the convertible and it rained. I was distracted on the computer and I didn't notice. The windows aren't working and the car's drenched. I feel awful. I'm really sorry."

There was a painfully long silence.

"Wow," he said. "I'm stunned. I don't know what to say."

It took him a few days to get over his shock and disappointment, and it took me a little longer to release my guilt and regret. That's life. We make mistakes. Our partners forgive us and we forgive ourselves. It's all okay.

The car dried out, though the windows still glitch on occasion. But luckily, I don't feel shame and self-judgment every time they do, anymore. Since I shared my mistake honestly when I needed to, it didn't fester, and it didn't become a bigger deal than it had to be.

Monogamy and Beyond

— Affairs
(Radcliff & Dahlia)

— Resilient Monogamy
(Peggie & Victor)

— Polyamory
(Darrel, Liz, & Mona)

> We are never safe from our own fantasy of hermetically sealed, perfect love.

48

Affairs

Radcliff was the one who called me about setting up a session. He used to live near my office, although now he lived alone in an apartment, 30 minutes away. Dahlia still lived in their old townhouse. Making it to our sessions would be a short commute, for her.

"The relationship is done for me," she said at our first session.

"Why do you think you're here?" I asked.

Dahlia made a conscious effort to look neutral, yet something else shined through her eyes, a mixture of hurt, longing, and doubt.

"To understand how he could do this. Right after my diagnosis."

Dahlia had been diagnosed with cancer a few months before Radcliff's affair. He'd driven her to her chemotherapy treatments, then driven her home, where she slept for hours at a time. During these recovery periods, Radcliff began to leave the house "to get some air." It was during one of these absences that Dahlia uncovered a salacious text thread between Radcliff and an ex-girlfriend referencing a recent sexual encounter.

"It didn't mean anything," Radcliff said. "I wish I could convince you."

"You can't," Dahlia said. "Being sick is hard enough, and then to find out you're screwing one of your exes while my hair's falling out and I'm puking in the toilet?"

In her book *The New Monogamy: Redefining Your Relationship after Infidelity*, relationship expert and sexologist Tammy Nelson, PhD, explores three phases of affair recovery: the crisis phase, the insight phase, and the vision phase. Couples in the crisis phase are recovering from the shock of the affair and the strong emotions it often triggers. In the insight phase, couples collaborate on understanding how the affair happened, how certain events and their conscious or unconscious behavior may have fed into the affair, and the affair's meaning. In the vision phase, couples begin to grow from the affair and make positive changes. A couple may decide to separate or divorce at this stage, or they may build a more conscious marriage.

For Dahlia and Radcliff, recovering from the affair was like being dropped into a dunking tank repeatedly and unpredictably. They might breathe a sigh of relief in the insight phase, glimpse the possibility of living together again in the vision phase, and then encounter a trigger that took them right back into crisis.

"I can't shake the thought that you were hoping I'd die," Dahlia said.

"You're wrong," Radcliff said. "It was horrible to see you sick."

"So you cheated on me to feel better?" Dahlia asked sarcastically.

In fact, this was partly true. In her book *The State of Affairs: Rethinking Infidelity*, popular author and sexuality expert Esther Perel writes about the frequent link between affairs and one of our most basic human fears: mortality. Radcliff had gone numb to cope with his own helplessness. He'd felt his own life draining out of him as he saw his wife withering. The affair had been an emotional defibrillator.

Dahlia saw the affair as a sign that her husband coped with difficulties in selfish and unhealthy ways. But, more than that, she couldn't get the notion out of her head that cheating had been a weapon he'd used, however unconsciously, to punish her for expecting more from him than he was able to give her and to distance himself from her neediness and fragility.

Affairs can indeed be weapons, but they're also skeleton keys. A skeleton or master key is one that can open many locks. An affair can function in the same way—opening doors to rooms couples have avoided entering over the course of a relationship, and maybe even of a lifetime: dusty rooms piled high with old fears and treasured, lost dreams, reviled or lost aspects of the self, and buried vulnerabilities.

Some couples decide it's worth it to enter these rooms and face what they find there. Other couples choose to leave the doors closed, turn away, and discard the key.

Exercise

The Speaker talks about their experience of an affair, either one they were involved in or one that affected them indirectly. Was it a weapon, a skeleton key, or something else? As the Speaker, talk about whether there were overt (or suspected) affairs in your family of origin. How have affairs impacted you? What have you learned from them?

Sample Exchange:

SPEAKER: My dad had several affairs. Nobody told me, but I still knew. Eventually he left my mom for his secretary. She never forgave him and used to tell me what a horrible person he was. It was hard because I loved my dad.

When I was in my twenties, one of my girlfriends cheated on me. In retrospect, I can see how going through her phone and questioning her all the time became a self-fulfilling prophecy. I never want to do that again. I want to give you space and trust you. Affairs have taught me you can't control people. It's scary to trust, but not trusting is even more damaging.

LISTENER: Thank you for being willing to talk about this. I want to keep talking about affairs rather than pretending they don't happen.

> Resilient monogamy is explicitly defined, flexible, and open for discussion.

49

Resilient Monogamy

Peggie and Victor were confused. They'd done everything right. They'd waited till their mid-thirties to get married. They'd each been in several relationships, experimented sexually, traveled the world, and immersed themselves in different cultures. They'd followed their passions and had their fair share of exhilarating, peak experiences before settling down.

"What in the world happened to us?" Peggie asked with a bitter smile. She'd taken off her flip-flops and pulled her legs up onto the chair in a meditator's pose. "We're so defeated."

Victor looked sad as he shrugged, turning his wedding ring around on his finger.

"Where's our passion?" Peggie asked. "Not just for each other—our passion for life?"

Their romantic trajectory had been exactly what every romance is supposed to be: They'd met on a work retreat, felt a strong attraction, dated, fallen in love, and gotten married. Within a few years, they'd had two children who were now in middle school.

"You want me in the house, so I stay in the house," Victor said defensively. "Then you get mad because I'm not really *present*. So I leave the house. Then you get mad because I left."

As a couple, they felt simultaneously satiated and deprived. They'd inhabited all the roles they were supposed to fill as parents, spouses, and professionals. They were behaving in responsible and predictable ways—in ways they'd learned, over the years, were the "right" ways to behave in a committed partnership. But what seemed "right" was turning out to be much too rigid for them.

In his article "Why Achieving Everything Can Make Your Life Worse," journalist Zat Rana points out that when we're overly focused on getting things right and on creating safety and predictability in our lives, we neglect the need for volatility. It seems counterintuitive, but we all need to nurture a zone of volatility in our lives. Rana references author and statistician Nassim Taleb's concept of "antifragility." Volatility can benefit a system by creating room for the movement needed to absorb shocks. Antifragility is often an overlooked measure of well-being in our lives and in our marriages.

Peggie and Victor hadn't talked much about what they needed from each other when they married, what their assumptions were, or how often they would revisit and update their expectations of one another as spouses moving forward. They'd moved from the delicious, temporary enmeshment of romantic love to the stability and commitment of a mature, responsible partnership. From there, they'd segued into their roles as parents: nesting, going to work, keeping their home running and their kids on track. They'd made all of these transitions without discussing what they needed to stay happy and fulfilled as unique human individuals. They'd sacrificed the volatility and antifragility that had once kept their relationship vibrant for certainty and predictability.

Despite the American ideology of self-determination, it's easy to conform to assumptions about what marriage is or should be. Taking on the task of cocreating a unique relational contract with our partners can feel like "reinventing the wheel." But it wasn't helping Peggie and Victor to operate under old, implicit agreements and assumptions from earlier on in their marriage. Their relationship was out of sync with their needs. Recognizing and prioritizing their desires, sharing them, and being able to make room for evolving desires meant questioning assumptions and renegotiating boundaries.

Couples therapist and sexologist Tammy Nelson, PhD, encourages couples to structure and update explicit monogamy agreements as their needs change and evolve in her book *The New Monogamy: Redefining Your Relationship after Infidelity*. A *resilient* monogamy agreement is cocreated, flexible, and explicit rather than assumed. Change doesn't destroy it, because it changes as a couple's needs change. A couple's faithfulness to maintaining ongoing honesty keeps this agreement current, giving partners room to grow.

Once we delved into this, Peggie and Victor were surprised by how many implicit assumptions and expectations they had of one another that weren't supportive of their updated passions, desire for adventure, and connection to others in their community. They saw and understood the need for a resilient monogamy agreement—one that allowed them to reconnect with their individual interests and autonomy. Their resilient monogamy agreement would include solo travel, time away from each other and the kids, and the freedom to rekindle old friendships and prioritize new ones.

Building a resilient monogamy reconnected them to their own lives and interests, and put them back onto a path of balance and ultimately reconnection with each other.

Exercise

Take a few minutes to look at potential areas in your resilient monogamy agreement, listed on the next two pages. Underline one area you'd like to explore, and circle three needs in that area. If you prefer, write down your area along with three needs.

The Speaker then shares their area, the implicit agreement they've been operating under, and their needs. Rather than blaming your partner for the implicit agreement, take psychological ownership (see chapter 11) and talk about your current needs from the heart. What will it take to create a conscious, resilient monogamy agreement in this area of your relationship?

Sample Exchange:

SPEAKER: My area is "family." I've been operating under an implicit monogamy agreement that because you and my sister don't get along, I shouldn't see her frequently or connect with her. My assumption has been that when people make a commitment to one another, they need to limit the family relationships their spouses don't approve of. It's been easier to avoid this than discuss it.

I'd like to connect with my sister more regularly and more often. I miss her. I want to spend quality time with her. I know you don't have a great relationship with her, but I would like you to get it to a better place, if possible. I would like her to come stay with us two or three times a year, or for you to be able to visit her with me—even if we stayed in a hotel rather than at her place. I'd like us both to keep our criticisms about family members to a minimum.

LISTENER: I appreciate your commitment to creating a conscious and resilient monogamy agreement that grows and evolves with us and our changing needs.

Resilient Monogamy Agreement Areas

TRAVEL	SOLITUDE	CREATIVITY	CHILDREN
More day trips	Time alone in house	Encouragement for my art	Having a child/ children
Traveling alone	Time alone out of house	Assistance with my art	Not having a child/children
Planning vacations	Time alone without you	Sharing my passion for art	Adopting a child/children
Travel with kids	Time alone with you	Creating things together	Focusing more on us
Travel together— just the two of us, without kids	Help creating alone time	Exploring our own creativity	Focusing more on our child/ children

EMOTIONAL CONNECTIONS	FAMILY	SEXUALITY
More connection with others	Seeing my family more	More exploration within our relationship
More emotional intimacy with others	Seeing my family less	More exploration outside of our relationship
Creating opportunities to connect with others	Seeing your family more	Sharing our fantasies and desires more
Your support connecting with others	Seeing your family less	Allowing for more sexual privacy and autonomy
I want *you* to connect with others	More approval of family	More sex education and experiential learning as a couple

Your Resilient Monogamy Area of Interest: _____

_____

Needs: _____

_____

_____

> Love is not an endless search or the hoarding of one treasure: it's a generative choice.

50

Polyamory

Six months ago, Darrel and Liz's relationship had undergone a radical change. They'd opened it up to another person: Mona. They came to see me because they wanted a nonjudgmental space to process some of the changes taking place between them. Experimenting with polyamory had pulled the rug out from under their world.

Darrel and Liz had considered themselves a happy couple. They loved each other deeply, communicated well, and had a warm and fulfilling sex life. Then, one night, their closest friends had shared the truth about their open relationship.

"We're faithful to each other, in full honesty and integrity," they had said. "But we're not faithful to cultural chastity belts."

Those words had resonated deeply with Liz. Although things were good with Darrel, she'd had a nagging feeling for quite some time that she wanted to explore another kind of arrangement.

"When they left, I told Darrel I really wanted to talk about opening things up," Liz said. "We'd been having conversations about polyamory for over a year, but they'd all been hypothetical. This was the first time I was serious about taking action."

Darrel shook his head as he remembered the shock of that moment. "I was scared. It sounded very risky to me. And it is risky."

Liz's eyes sparkled.

"Can you put words to your feelings, Liz?" I asked.

"I was scared, too," Liz said. "My entire adult life, I've had a lot of judgment about wanting to be with multiple partners. My previous partners took this as a sign that I didn't love them, or reacted with anger, and, eventually, I would just end up leaving my primary relationship and starting a new one."

"I know she loves me," Darrel said. "And I know I want to be with her. She's an explorer by nature. We're always going on wilderness hikes and traveling to places most people wouldn't go if you paid them. It's part of who she is."

"I'm proud of us," Liz said. "We've dealt with a lot, and a lot has changed. I haven't seen Mona for two weeks because she's asked for a little distance from all of this. But I do feel like Darrel and I are stronger as a couple. Weirdly, I feel even more committed."

In her book *Opening Up: A Guide to Creating and Sustaining Open Relationships*, Tristan Taormino warns couples against recklessly exploring polyamory or nonmonogamy. Being unhappy in your current relationship, dissatisfied with the sex, wanting to "fit in" or be on the cutting edge, seeking a sexual thrill with another person, fearing losing your partner if you don't go along with their desire for nonmonogamy—these are fragile motives for swimming out into the powerful undercurrents of polyamory, particularly within a culture that's structured for monogamy. Exploring a nonmonogamous lifestyle ethically and consensually takes self-awareness, maturity, and highly developed communication skills.

"I knew that the only way this had a chance of working would be if I continued to feel cared for and respected and like I was her number one," Darrel said. "And that meant we were talking about what was going on for each of us emotionally every step of the way."

"It was pretty painstaking," Liz said. "I'd go to a party, flirt with someone, and then come home and tell him about it. We were always cycling through so many emotions. We still are."

"We started gradually, with sharing a lot, and processing our reactions," Darrel said. "By the time she went to Burning Man and met Mona, it wasn't such a shock."

"Mona wasn't looking to be in a committed relationship. She wanted a lover and a lot of flexibility," Liz said.

But Liz and Darrel also admitted they'd been battered and bruised by the sudden, unexpected emotional turns they'd taken on their polyamorous ride so far.

"I get very scared," Liz said. "I long for Mona in a different way than I do for Darrel. He's a constant and Mona is elusive. It's hard on our marriage. Darrel feels taken for granted. Sometimes I worry that I'm gay and deluding myself by being with Darrel."

"It's a huge blow to your ego, seeing your wife excited by another person," Darrel said. "When all this started, I thought Liz having a female lover wouldn't be a threat to me, as if me and my penis would somehow still be the center of the universe. Boy, was I wrong."

Honestly evaluating your beliefs about monogamy, love, sex, relationship structures, emotional risk and safety, and sexual pleasure is critical if you and your partner are interested in exploring nonmonogamy. Darrel and Liz admitted that in the last six months alone, they'd wanted to unbuckle and get off the polyamory roller coaster many times. Despite their bond and respect for one another, they'd inadvertently hurt each other and Mona in ways they hadn't been able to forsee or prevent. Being ethical, transparent, and clear about desires and boundaries hadn't saved them from painful misunderstandings and powerful emotional reactions.

"The way I see it, people who are unhappy in their monogamous relationships hurt each other, too," Liz said. "At least we're living the way we want to, full-throttle, authentically and openly."

"When I'm not caught up in my fears or my wounded pride," Darrel said, "I can feel very relaxed about things. I get that she's with me because she wants to be. It's really her choice."

They'd experienced powerful shifts and changes that were expanding their sense of themselves, each other, and their possibility in the world. Their detour off the road of traditional monogamy and sexual exclusivity had unraveled many of their unquestioned narratives about attraction, sexual identity, pleasure, and marriage. But it had also created new unanswered questions.

"What if Darrel decides he wants a lover?" Liz asked me during one of our sessions.

"We'd navigate it together," Darrel said.

For many couples, simply talking about polyamory generates a sense of excitement, freedom, and sexual aliveness. It can remind couples that they are free to choose one another every day, free to be together in ways that work for both of them, and free to keep their partnership boundaries either consciously open or consciously closed.

Although the thought of exploring multiple lovers may be scary, it can also feel invigorating. Even if polyamory isn't for you as a couple, slightly loosening the grip of an inherited, many-centuries-deep, culturally enforced sexual-exclusivity taboo can release a lot of pent-up psychic, emotional, and sexual energy. It can open you and your partner up to appreciating one another in a new way.

Exercise

The Speaker shares one of their desires and one of their fears related to the idea of polyamory. Some questions to think about: Can you imagine your partner being sexual with someone other than you? Do you struggle to handle strong feelings like jealousy and fear? Are you emotionally available to your current partner? Do you have excess energy to invest in cultivating and working on multiple sexually intimate relationships? Do you have clear boundaries with people, and do you communicate your needs directly?

Sample Exchange:

SPEAKER: I really like the idea of talking with you about what would turn us on with other people. I'd like to create a bucket list of sexual experiences we could potentially choose to have together, things we could do or might consider doing at some point, which we could number from 1–20 with one being the least "out-there" thing we could try as a couple and 20 being the most "out-there" thing we can imagine doing. I think number 20 for me would be going to a sex club and watching another woman seduce you. I can definitely imagine you having sex with someone else. The thought of that makes me queasy, but it also turns me on. I don't know if it would in reality, though.

One of my fears is that one of us will fall in love with someone else and I'll lose you.

LISTENER: Thank you for sharing one of your desires related to polyamory with me. I'm grateful we can talk about this, and explore ideas like this openly together.

stepping stone
BEING "ALL-IN"

Commitment means being "all-in." It can sometimes feel like being "all-in" isn't a safe choice, and maybe sometimes it isn't. If that's the case, and safety is truly an issue, then you need to get yourself "all-out." A couple means two, not one and three quarters. This doesn't mean you should blindly commit to relationships that aren't good for you. Paradoxically, though, a relationship has no chance of being good for you if you're not in it. When you take your partner as they are, you take them with their flawed beliefs, with the ways they process information, with their social gaffes and bad habits, and with their changing body.

If you've ever ridden a motorcycle as a driver or a passenger with another person, you know the challenge of navigating smoothly on two wheels. There's a commitment required. Being aware of the rules of the road, of the need for quick reflexes, defensive-driving skills, and extra caution is critical, whether you're on a Greek island or the Brooklyn Bridge. At the same time, driver and passenger need to be *on* the bike together. If someone isn't committed to the ride you're taking—but gets on anyway—it's risky. If you have one foot sticking out in the air; if you're ready to jump off at the potholes; if you doubt yourself, each other, the road, or the motorcycle, the ride becomes unpleasant at best and risky at worst. Even if you try your best to compensate for one another's fears, poor attunement, or unpredictable body-weight distribution, the ride remains wobbly and dangerous.

Being partially committed isn't sustainable.

Think of your relationship like that motorcycle ride. Are you in or out? On or off? You can't be both. When you commit to a relationship without fully committing to it—internally hedging your bets, hoping and waiting for your partner to change, telling yourself you'll invest more later, after you have the proof you're looking for that this is the right choice—you're not committed at all. You're sabotaging your own ride.

General Inspiration

— Loving Imperfectly
   (Radcliff & Dahlia)

— Celebrating Life Together
   (Elly & Sebastian)

The road to
heaven is paved with
imperfection.

51

Loving
Imperfectly

Radcliff and Dahlia, from chapter 48, continued moving through the crisis, insight, and vision phases of affair recovery. There were many sessions when simply showing up and being in the room together with some modicum of kindness, hope, and respect was an achievement. Dahlia's cancer was in full remission, but she still felt listless. Working on their relationship after the affair was a double-edged sword—it increased her attachment to Radcliff and also felt humiliating. In some ways, it would have been easier to separate.

Radcliff and Dahlia explored what had happened, not only over the course of Radcliff's affair and her illness, but decades before that. The metaphor of the affair as a "skeleton key" resonated with them. A key can be held by both people in a relationship, whereas "an affair" had locked Dahlia and Radcliff into victim/perpetrator positions.

When Dahlia "held" the skeleton key, she used it to take psychological ownership, see her projections, and recognize just how much she had judged, demanded, nitpicked, and criticized Radcliff over the years. She hadn't considered the cumulative impact on him of being given the message, over and over again, that he wasn't loving her the way she wanted to be loved. She'd complained about his touch, his smell, the way he walked up the stairs, the way he loaded the dishwasher, his driving, and even the way he chewed his food. She also recognized that many of her frustrations with Radcliff had been red herrings, front-and-center distractions from the scarier work of experiencing her own fear of being viewed as unlovable.

"I was so busy looking for perfection I think I ended up pushing you away," Dahlia said in one of her more self-reflective moments.

"I don't want you blaming yourself," Radcliff said weakly.

"I'm not," Dahlia said. "I'm trying to see the bigger picture."

Radcliff looked dizzy, like he'd climbed a mountain and the oxygen at this height was hard to take in. "Thank you."

In the wake of the affair, Dahlia faced the ways she'd turned away from Radcliff's love for years. In her obsessive focus on the things about him that could use improvement, she'd failed to receive the imperfect love he'd been offering her all along.

In his book *Finding Meaning in an Imperfect World*, Iddo Landau, PhD, a professor of philosophy, challenges the perfectionism we're raised with, the constant push toward unparalleled romantic love, stellar successes, grand achievements, and excellence. He calls into question the values of perfectionists, who don't see the good in what's real or the value of what's not perfect. When you're too busy prioritizing an illusion, you miss out on what's right in front of you.

Gradually, Dahlia softened into her own grief, some of it related to the affair, but much of it connected to her past as a lonely girl with a stage mother who'd ushered her from one audition to the next in her push to vicariously experience stardom. Dahlia had grown up believing she had to be perfect to be loved. She'd carried this perfectionism into her relationship with Radcliff.

During one of our last sessions, Radcliff volunteered to be the first to share an appreciation of Dahlia. He opened his mouth to speak, then blinked and swallowed.

"I appreciate that you cleared out half the bedroom closet," he said at last, "and made space for my toiletries in the medicine cabinet."

Immediately, he bowed his head and his shoulders rose and fell rhythmically. Dahlia's face grew tender, a mixture of sorrow and joy.

"I'm just glad," Radcliff said. "I don't know why I'm getting emotional."

Dahlia touched his leg. Radcliff clasped her hand.

Loving imperfectly is a revolutionary act. It means we're agents in creating our relational world rather than passive judges finding fault with the imperfect love our partners give us. When we can lean into the imperfect love in ourselves and in our partners, we generate more love. It's how we heal ourselves and our marriages.

Exercise

Using the following lists, the Speaker shares two Perfect Love Expectations along with two Imperfect Love Mantras. How does it feel to own up to your Perfect Love Expectations? How do you think these Perfect Love Expectations impact your partner? How does it feel to imagine adopting your Imperfect Love Mantras and loving your partner from this new perspective?

Sample Exchange:

SPEAKER: My Perfect Love Expectations are, "If it's not what I want, I can't accept it," and, "If you loved me, you'd know what I need and give it to me." My Imperfect Love Mantras are, "I can trust your heart and accept your offerings as they are," and, "You won't always know what I need or give me what I need."

It feels humbling to own up to my Perfect Love Expectations. I imagine it's hard for you when I impose my Perfect Love Expectations on you. When I imagine adopting my Imperfect Love Mantras as a new way of thinking about love, I feel vulnerable. The idea of trusting my heart and of accepting your offerings even when they're not exactly what I want scares me.

LISTENER: Thank you for sharing your Perfect Love Expectations and your Imperfect Love Mantras. It means a lot to me that you can take responsibility for these expectations and imagine living from a different mind-set.

PERFECT LOVE EXPECTATIONS	IMPERFECT LOVE MANTRAS
If it's not what I want, I can't accept it.	I can trust your heart and accept your offerings as they are.
I need to stay mad, withdraw my love, punish you, or prove I'm right.	I can soften into vulnerability and trust us.
I can't accept your love fully until you change.	I can accept your love fully whether or not you change according to my agenda.
Real love is fluid and easy.	Real love can be tumultuous.
Real love always "holds me."	Real love makes room for loneliness.
Real love never lets go.	Real love gives space and freedom.
Real love is always connected.	Real love makes room for inevitable disconnection.
If you loved me, you'd know what I needed and give it to me.	Even loving me, you won't always give me what I need.

Couples who
celebrate life create lives
worth celebrating.

52

Celebrating Life Together

Exploring dishonesty brought Elly and Sebastian (see chapter 46) face-to-face with another challenge many couples struggle with: the challenge of celebrating life.

In America, productivity reigns. Success and achievement are unquestioned cultural expectations. Celebrating just to celebrate can seem like a waste of energy and time. When we try to celebrate our lives, there's often a nagging voice at the back of our minds, saying, "You could be *doing* something." Why would we stop to celebrate? What nonsense. Life's too short.

Maybe it is, and yet it's also too short *not* to celebrate. And for couples, celebration is the sweetness of love expressed. It's both curative care and preventive medicine.

"It's been interesting observing myself," Sebastian said. He had been bringing mindfulness to his truth-bending tendencies, particularly with Elly, and had started making a habit of Radical Honesty Shares (see page 226). "The things I used to lie about—the things I still *want* to lie about—most of them have to do with celebrating life. Whenever I'm happy, or excited, or just grateful, I look for a way to mark the moment. My first impulse is to buy something: a pricey bottle of wine or an expensive cigar, a first-class ticket on a business trip, a designer suit, or a pair of gold-plated cuff links."

"You enjoy celebrating special moments?" I was trying to follow his lead.

"There was no celebration for me growing up," Sebastian said as if that explained it. "My mother had Lou Gehrig's disease. No one told me not to be happy, but enjoying things and celebrating life felt weirdly wrong. It feels wrong to celebrate anything when you're a kid and your mother is dying."

Elly listened intently, absorbing this new information.

"I felt guilty a lot. Even just being healthy when she wasn't," Sebastian admitted. "I started shoplifting, stealing toys, candy, baseball cards. When I stole things, I could celebrate quietly and also feel bad, because I knew I'd done something wrong."

"Getting things to celebrate and feeling guilty," Elly said. "Like when you buy hundred-dollar cigars, rack up debt and lie about it."

"Yes, like that," Sebastian agreed.

As a boy caught between aliveness and a dying mother, he'd found ways to celebrate that defeated celebration.

Even if you didn't grow up with Sebastian's internal struggle or external circumstances, you may notice a tendency to undermine your own joy and celebratory impulses throughout the day. Elly and Sebastian recognized that they needed to change their approach to celebrating the good in their lives. It couldn't be conditional—a reward at the end of the month or something they'd suffered for or "earned." They began to celebrate life randomly, just because. They were alive, they were together, and life was worth celebrating—every day.

There's a quality of gritty adoration, of tender mischievousness, to the interactions of celebratory couples. Even if they're facing challenges, their eyes sparkle. When partners *don't* celebrate life, this energy wanes. There's an extra layer of effort in just waking up and going about the ordinary business of living. Couples who embrace the countercultural importance of unjustified, irrational celebration—and do so unapologetically and often—lead lives worth celebrating.

Exercise

Love Catch is one way to celebrate together while simultaneously engaging in the important business of silliness. Find an appropriate object—a tennis ball, a beanbag, or a tangerine. You'll be tossing your object back and forth in your Couples Spot.

Once your Love Catch begins, focus on calling out, "I celebrate . . ." and completing the sentence with whatever comes to mind. Dropping the ball, feeling goofy, not knowing what to say, and laughing are signs you're doing this exercise correctly. Don't worry if it doesn't feel comfortable. Be ready to try this exercise more than once. Playing and celebrating with our partners can be one of the hardest skills for couples to master.

Sample Exchange:

SPEAKER: I celebrate our life together!

LISTENER: I celebrate your eyes!

SPEAKER: I celebrate your cooking!

LISTENER: I celebrate your hot body!

SPEAKER: I celebrate dancing!

LISTENER: I celebrate your job promotion!

SPEAKER: I celebrate your smile!

LISTENER: I celebrate making out with you!

SPEAKER: I celebrate eating ice cream!

LISTENER: I celebrate your generosity!

SPEAKER: I celebrate our health!

LISTENER: I celebrate your sense of humor!

SPEAKER: Thank you for playing Love Catch with me. It felt silly and good. I liked hearing you give a voice to the things you celebrate.

LISTENER: I'm glad you're celebrating with me, too. Doing this reminded me of everything we already have that's worth being joyful about. It loosened me up.

Stepping Stone
SUSTAINABLE LOVE

Love relies on our small, everyday choices for sustainability. The right tools, awareness, commitment, and a healthy dose of humility can help us see the bigger picture in our relationships in the midst of searing comments, neglectful actions, recurring oversights, or a hurtful look or tone of voice. It's this view to sustainability that allows the seedlings of romantic love to grow strong and resilient.

One of the ironies of many self-help books is that they're here to encourage you to connect with the part of you that doesn't need self-help books. Just as good therapists work themselves out of a job, as you have completed these chapters and exercises, you may notice that your original need for what's contained within them has lessened. If it hasn't, or if the need arises again, you can always turn to the couples in these chapters for motivation, inspiration, or just as a reminder of the universality of the struggles we all go through in our desire to fight less and cultivate sustainable love.

Resources and References

Bradberry, Travis, and Jean Greaves. *Emotional Intelligence 2.0.* TalentSmart, 2009.

Brown, Brené. *Daring Greatly: How the Courage to Be Vulnerable Transforms the Way We Live, Love, Parent, and Lead.* Avery, 2015.

Chödrön, Pema. *When Things Fall Apart: Heart Advice for Difficult Times.* Shambala Library, 2002.

Cline, Foster, and Jim Fay. *Parenting with Love and Logic: Teaching Children Responsibility.* Navpress, 2006.

DiClemente, Carlo. *Addiction and Change: How Addictions Develop and Addicted People Recover*, second edition. The Guilford Press, 2018.

Ellis, Albert. *How to Stubbornly Refuse to Make Yourself Miserable About Anything (Yes, Anything!).* Citadel Press, 1988, 2006.

Fosha, Diana. *The Transforming Power of Affect: A Model for Accelerated Change.* Basic Books, 2000.

Gendlin, Eugene T. *Focusing.* Bantam Books, 1978.

Gottman, John. The Gottman Couples Retreat Board Game. Gott Facts Card. 2014.

Gottman, John, and Nan Silver. *The Seven Principles for Making Marriage Work*, revised. Harmony, 2015: pp. 25–46.

Greenspan, Stanley. *Playground Politics: Understanding the Emotional Life of Your School-Age Child.* Addison Wesley, 1993.

Hendricks, Gay. *The Big Leap: Conquer Your Hidden Fear and Take Life to the Next Level.* Harper, 2009.

Hendrix, Harville. *Getting the Love You Want: A Guide for Couples.* Twentieth Anniversary Edition. Henry Holt, 2008.

Hendrix, Harville, and Helen LaKelly Hunt. *Receiving Love: Transform Your Relationship by Letting Yourself Be Loved.* Atria Books, 2004.

Kornfield, Jack. *The Art of Forgiveness, Lovingkindness, and Peace.* Bantam Books, 2002.

Landau, Iddo. *Finding Meaning in an Imperfect World.* Oxford University Press, 2017.

Lerner, Harriet. *The Dance of Anger: A Woman's Guide to Changing the Patterns of Intimate Relationships*. Perennial Currents, 2005.

Mellody, Pia. *Facing Codependence: What It Is, Where It Comes From, How It Sabotages Our Lives*. Harper & Row, 2003.

Meyer, Pamela. *Liespotting: Proven Techniques to Detect Deception*. St. Martin's Press, 2010.

Nagoski, Emily. *Come as You Are: The Surprising New Science That Will Transform Your Sex Life*. Simon & Schuster, 2015.

Nelson, Tammy. *The New Monogamy: Redefining Your Relationship after Infidelity*. New Harbinger Publications, 2012.

Perel, Esther. *The State of Affairs: Rethinking Infidelity*. Harper, 2017.

Real, Terrence. *How Can I Get Through to You? Closing the Intimacy Gap Between Men and Women*. Simon & Schuster, 2002.

Rilke, Rainer Maria. *Letters to a Young Poet*. New World Library, 2000.

Schwartz, Richard C. *Introduction to the Internal Family Systems Model*. Trailheads, 2001.

Shahbaz, Caroline, and Peter Chirinos. *Becoming a Kink Aware Therapist*. Routledge, 2017.

Siegel, Daniel. *Mindsight: The New Science of Personal Transformation*. Reprint edition. Bantam, 2010.

Siegel, Daniel, and Tiny Payne Bryson. *The Whole-Brain Child: 12 Revolutionary Strategies to Nurture Your Child's Developing Mind*. Bantam Books, 2012.

Steiner-Adair, Catherine. *The Big Disconnect: Protecting Childhood and Family Relationships in the Digital Age*. Harper, 2013.

Taormino, Tristan. *Opening Up: A Guide to Creating and Sustaining Open Relationships*. Cleis Press, 2008.

Tatkin, Stan. *Wired for Love: How Understanding Your Partner's Brain and Attachment Style Can Help You Defuse Conflict and Build a Secure Relationship*. New Harbinger Publications, 2011.

Thomashauer, Regina. *Pussy: A Reclamation*. Hay House, 2016.

Tsabary, Shefali. *The Awakened Family: A Revolution in Parenting*. Viking, 2016.

van der Kolk, Bessel. *The Body Keeps the Score: Brain, Mind, and Body in the Healing of Trauma*. Penguin Books, 2014.

Weinhold, Barry, and Janae Weinhold. *How to Break Free of the Drama Triangle and Victim Consciousness*. CreateSpace, 2014.

Online Articles and Websites

ASAM (American Society of Addiction Medicine). "Public Policy Statement Short Definition of Addiction." Accessed July 18, 2018. https://www.asam.org/docs/default-source /public-policy-statements/1definition_of_addiction_short_4-11 .pdf?sfvrsn=6e36cc2_0.

Erotic Blueprint Quiz website. Accessed August 8, 2018. http://www.eroticbreakthrough.com.

Femme! Accessed September 2, 2018. http://www.livefemme.com.

The Focusing Institute. Accessed on September 1, 2018. http://www.focusing.org/sixsteps.html.

Fries, Dan. "The Benefits of Thinking Scarce." Accessed June 22, 2018. https://danfries.net/scarcity.

Gottman, John. "How to Build Trust." Accessed July 28, 2018. https://www.youtube.com/watch?v=rgWnadSi91s.

Harvard Medical School. "Understanding the Stress Response." Accessed July 17, 2018. Harvard Health Publishing. https://www.health.harvard.edu/staying-healthy/understanding -the-stress-response.

Hirschhorn, Deb. Goodtherapy.org. Accessed July 20, 2018. https://www.goodtherapy.org/blog/little-white-lies-how -dishonesty-affects-intimate-relationships-0720174.

Imago Relationships International. Accessed June 1, 1018. http://imagorelationships.org/pub/about-imago-therapy /imago-dialogue-101.

Mills, Harry, Natalie Reiss, Mark Dombeck. MentalHelp.net. 2008. Accessed June 24, 2018. https://www.mentalhelp.net/articles /types-of-stressors-eustress-vs-distress.

Powell, John A., and Stephen Menendian. Othering and Belonging; Expanding the Circle of Human Concern. "The Problem of Othering: Towards Inclusiveness and Belonging." Accessed June 20, 2018. http://www.otheringandbelonging.org/the -problem-of-othering.

Ramsay, Douglas, and Stephen Woods. NCBI. "Clarifying the Roles of Homeostasis and Allostasis in Physiological Regulation. " Accessed September 4, 2018. https://www.ncbi.nlm.nih.gov/pmc /articles/PMC4166604.

Rana, Zat. "Why Achieving Everything Can Make Your Life Worse." Accessed July 30, 2018. https://medium.com/personal-growth /why-getting-everything-you-want-can-make-your-life-worse -9b32671c4ea0.

Rodgers, Joann Ellison. "Go Forth in Anger." *Psychology Today*. 2014. Accessed June 14, 2018. https://www.psychologytoday.com/us /articles/201403/go-forth-in-anger.

Sell, Aaron. Center for Evolutionary Psychology. Accessed July 10, 2018. https://www.cep.ucsb.edu/grads/Sell/Research.html.

Sills, Judith. "The Power of No." November, 2013. *Psychology Today*. Accessed June 10, 2018. https://www.psychologytoday.com/us /articles/201311/the-power-no.

Thomashauer, Regena. "The 4 Keys to an Extraordinary Life." Accessed on June 23, 2018. http://mamagenas.com/4-keys-to-an -extraordinary-life.

World Health Organization. Accessed July 18, 2018. http://www.who.int/reproductivehealth/topics/gender_rights /sexual_health/en.

Index

A

ABC Model for stress, 161
Abundance mind-set, 85–88
Abuse, xix
Accelerated experiential dynamic
    psychotherapy (AEDP), 13
Addiction and Change
    (DiClemente), 216
Addictions, 214–217
Affairs, 229–231
Alliance, 79
Ambiversion, 93
American Society of Addiction
    Medicine, 215
Anger, 130–133
Antifragility, 233
Appreciations, 65–68
*Art of Forgiveness, Lovingkindness and
    Peace* (Kornfield), 147

B

Baer, Greg, 111
Becoming a Kink Aware Therapist
    (Shahbaz and Chirinos), 210
Behavior Change Request Dialogue, 93
Being right, 141–144
Big Disconnect, The (Steiner-Adair), 215
Big Leap, The (Hendricks), 158
Blended families, 175–178
Body Keeps the Score, The
    (van der Kolk), 135
Boundaries, 45
    money, 154–157
Bradberry, Travis, 92
Brown, Brené, 40

C

Celebrating life, 249–252
Chapman, Gary, 187
Check-ins, 57–60
Chirinos, Peter, 210
Chödrön, Pema, 142
Cline, Foster, 172
Closeness, 79
Cognitive behavioral therapy (CBT), 135
Collaboration, 120–123
Come as You Are (Nagoski), 200
Commitment, 243
Communication stoppers, 24
"Comparison Level for Alternatives"
    (CLalt), 124, 223
Concretizing, 142
Conflict, 126–129
Contempt, 127
Convictions, 143–144
Counterdependency, 105–108.
    See also Dependency
Couples Spot, xx–xxi
Couples Time Container, xx–xxi, xxiii
Criticism, 127

D

Dance of Anger, The (Lerner), 131
Daring Greatly (Brown), 40
Decision-making, 120–123
Defenses, 13
Defensiveness, 127
Dependency, 101–104. *See also*
    Counterdependency
Desire discrepancy, 198–202
DiClemente, Carlo, 216
Dishonesty, 218–221
Distress, 161–163, 169

Drama Triangle, 180–182
Dyer, Wayne, 142

E
Ebbinghaus illusion, 86, 88
"Einstein Time," 158
Ellis, Albert, 161
Emotional Intelligence 2.0 (Bradberry
	and Greaves), 92
Empathy, 29–31, 32
Erotic Blueprints, 208–211
Eustress, 160–163, 169
Expressive movement, 184
Extroversion, 92–93
Eye-gazing, 35, 37

F
Facing Codependence (Mellody), 45
Fay, Jim, 172
Feelings, 12–15, 114
	anger, 130–133
	and expressive movement, 184
Fighting, 138–139
Fight response, 165–168
Finding Meaning in an Imperfect World
	(Landau), 246
Five Love Languages (Chapman), 187
Flight response, 165–168
"Floortime" concept, 176–177
Focusing, 148
Forgiveness, 145–147
Fosha, Diana, 13
Four Horsemen patterns of
	interaction, 127
Freeze response, 165–168
Friendships, 95–98

G
Gender roles, 116–119
Gendlin, Eugene T., 148
Gottman, John, 66, 124, 127
Gratitude, 65–68
Greaves, Jean, 92
Greenspan, Stanley, 176–177

Ground rules, xxiv
GULPs (Give Unconditional Love
	Plans), 111–113

H
Hendricks, Gay, 158
Hendrix, Harville, 21, 32
Honesty, 226–227. *See also* Dishonesty
How Can I Get Through to You?
	(Real), 139
Hunt, Helen LaKelly, 21, 32

I
Imago Dialogue, 21, 27, 32
Imago Relationship Therapy, 21
	Behavior Change Request
		Dialogue, 93
	To-Do Love Lists (TDLs), 192–195
	Imago Dialogue, 21, 27, 32
	Parent-Child Dialogue, 73
Imperfection, 245–248
Imperfect Love Mantras, 247–248
Inferiority, 71–74
Infidelity, 229–231
In-laws, 179–183
Inner orphan, 75–78
Internal Family Systems, 76–77
Interoception, 135
Intimacy, 34–37, 42
Introversion, 92–93

J
Jaiya, 199, 209
Jealousy, 75–78
Jung, Carl, 92

K
Karpman, Stephe, 180
Kornfield, Jack, 147

L
Landau, Iddo, 246
Lerner, Harriet, 131
Liespotting (Meyer), 220

Listener role, xxi
Listening, 20–23, 148
Love Catch, 251–252
Love languages
    To-Do Love Lists (TDLs), 192–195
    identifying, 186–188
    speaking your partner's, 189–191
Love rituals, 59
Lying, 218–221

M
Mellody, Pia, 45
Mental illness, xix
Meyer, Pamela, 220
Mindfulness, 135
Mindsight, 162
Mirroring, 21, 32
Money
    boundaries, 154–157
    meanings of, 150–153
Monogamy, resilient, 232–237

N
Nagoski, Emily, 200
Needs, satisfying, 44–47, 99
Negative survival bias, 67
Nelson, Tammy, 230, 234
New Monogamy, The (Nelson), 230, 234
"No," saying, 6–9

O
Opening Up (Taormino), 239
Oxygen-mask metaphor, 3

P
Parent-Child Dialogue, 73
Parenting
    blended families, 176–177
    styles, 171–174
Parenting with Love and Logic
        (Cline and Fay), 172
Perception filters, 86
Perel, Esther, 230
Perfect Love Expectations, 247–248

Perspective, 85–89
Pleasant, Bernadette, 184
Polyamory, 238–242
Projection, 52–54
Pseudo adult, 77–78
Psychological ownership, 48–51

R
Radical Honesty Shares, 226–227
Rana, Zat, 233
Reactivity, 69
Real, Terry, 139
Real Love (Baer), 111
Re-dos, 142–143
Reentries, 61–64
Relationships
    benefits, 224–225
    blended families, 175–178
    friendships, 95–98
    gender roles in, 116–119
    in-laws, 179–183
    polyamory, 238–242
Remorse, 145–147
Resilient monogamy, 232–237
Respect, 126–129

S
Safety, 89
Satisfaction, 222–224
Scarcity mind-set, 85–88
Schwartz, Richard, 76
Self-care, 2–5, 10
Self-esteem, 71–74
Sell, Aaron, 131–132
Sexuality
    definitions of, 212
    desire discrepancy, 198–202
    Erotic Blueprints, 208–211
    polyamory, 238–242
    shame, 203–207
Shahbaz, Caroline, 210
Shame, sexual, 203–207
Sherrington, Charles S., 135
"Shoulds," 44–47

Siegel, Dan, 162
Sills, Judith, 7
"Skeleton key" metaphor, 245–246
Slepian, Carol Kramer, 142
SMART requests, 93
Social exchange theory, 223
Speaker role, xxi
State of Affairs, The (Perel), 230
Steiner-Adair, Catherine, 215
Stepping Stones, xxii
    Being "All-In," 243
    Communication Stoppers, 24
    Compare and Despair, 124
    From Distress to Eustress, 169
    Huddle, 79
    Imago Dialogue, 32
    Infinite Universes, 89
    Intimacy Comfort Levels, 42
    It's Already Happening, 196
    Messengers in Disguise, 114
    Move It, 184
    Radical Honesty Shares, 226–227
    Self-Care, 10
    Sensation is Information, 148
    Sustainable Love, 253
    Tandem Emotional Mountain
      Climbing, 69
    Time Management, 158
    Vent Boxes, 55
    What's in a Word, 212
    What to Do Mid-Fight, 138–139
    What You Need to Receive, I Need
      to Give, 99
Stonewalling, 127–128

Stories, 16–19
Stress
    eustress vs. distress, 160–163, 169
    responses to, 164–168
Superiority, 71–74
Sustainability, 253

T
Takeoffs, 61–64
Taleb, Nassim, 233
Taormino, Tristan, 239
Tatkin, Stan, 61–62
Thomashauer, Regena, 14
Time management, 158
Transitions, 61–64
Triggers, 134–137
True adult, 77–78

U
Unconditional love, 109–113

V
Validation, 26–28, 32
Values, 81–84
van der Kolk, Bessel, 135
Vent Boxes, 55
Vulnerability, 38–41

W
When Things Fall Apart (Chödrön), 142
Wired for Love (Tatkin), 62

Y
"Yes," saying, 6–9

Acknowledgments

Tammy Nelson, who could easily sit on her laurels and hoard her wisdom, has chosen instead to share it with me and others. Who knew one woman could have so many gifts? Thank you for your writing and publishing savvy; for your authenticity, generosity and humor; and for helping me find and use my voice. Inara de Luna—your name says it all. I'm over-the-moon grateful for the many ways you held down the fort while I wrote this book.

The editors who have appeared in my life over the past year and a half have supported me in ways they're likely not even remotely aware of: Rob Wieman at Goodtherapy.org for urging me to keep writing; Marthine Satris for reading and liking my blog; Livia Kent at the *Psychotherapy Networker* for picking up the phone and being so open to reading my work; and Pippa White, for her editorial elegance in what has been a supremely seamless and pleasurable collaboration.

I've had such powerful mentorship in the writers, psychotherapists, and powerhouse thinkers whose books I've read over the years, many of whom I've referenced in these pages. Thank you for living large and for your own unique alchemy of language and passion.

I'm grateful to The School of Womanly Arts and Regena Thomashauer for introducing me to critical information that was missing from my formal education, and for giving me the opportunity to cultivate friendships that formed a chrysalis around me over the past year as I gestated this book. Thank you, Po-Hong Yu, for your fierce friendship at every twist and turn of this process. Kanelli Scalcoyannis, Justine Klineman, Carrie Silver, Aman Gohal, Tyra Sammons-Lane, Meenal Kelkar, Linda Yablonski, Linda Harter, Kadedra Spruill, Stephanie Redlener, Heather Drummond, Anne-Laure Fleurie, Kimberly Baker Simms, Christina Martin, Rumena Turkedjiev, Swandala Dennis-Jones, Leora Edut, Trudy Miller, Tsipa Swan, Racquel Cousins Paytas, April Amodeo, Andrea Anderson and *all* the 2018 Creationistas: thank you for being "all in."

Nerina Garcia-Arcement, having you as a friend and colleague from our externship days at Bellevue Hospital into private practice, has been my umbilical cord to community when I have felt isolated. Thank you for your brilliant mind, huge heart, and therapist's intuition.

Jennifer Charles, Leslie Bumstead, Deborah Poynton, Greg Jones, Wendy Kagan, Lee Bob Black, Ute Lichterfeld, Inna Topiler Mooney, Sue Varma, Nataliya Rusetskaya, Lauren Zehner, and you too, Bébé—you've enriched my life with years of support, laughter and connection and I'm thrilled for this opportunity to acknowledge you for it.

A bucketload of appreciation also goes to my mother Pat Muñoz for living fearlessly and fully, and to my brother John, for his integrity and benevolence—I'm blessed you're family.

I'm beyond grateful to my son, Lucas, for tolerating my double standards when I indulged in too much screen time writing this book. It's been my own brand of heaven on earth to look up and see you sitting across from me all summer long, immersed in books of your own as you generously shared your popsicles.

Mike, you're everything I've ever wanted in a partner, and more. You've never, ever doubted me and what I'm capable of, and you've talked me off the ledge of my writer's anxieties for well over a decade. I'm so lucky to have you as a co-conspirator in life, parenthood, and all that lies beyond. You've rocked my world and been my rock. I couldn't have done this growing-up-and-being-fully-alive thing without you.

My gratitude to my clients knows no bounds. Thank you for choosing to work with me, to move forward through the undertow of the past, and to affirm life by affirming your life.

About the Author

Alicia Muñoz is a Virginia, New Jersey, and New York State Licensed Professional Counselor and desire expert, based in Falls Church, Virginia. She earned her master's degree from New York University in Mental Health and Wellness Counseling and her postgraduate certification in Imago Relationship Therapy. She has also received extensive training in accelerated experiential dynamic psychotherapy (AEDP). Prior to opening her private practice, Alicia provided individual, couples, and group therapy at Bellevue Hospital's World Trade Center Mental Health Program. Passionate about sustainable love, Alicia shares her views on the power of committed relationships through her blog, as well as print and online magazines like *Counseling Today*, GoodTherapy.org, YourTango.com, and *Psychotherapy Networker*. She lives in Virginia with her husband and son. Learn more and sign up for her free newsletter with tips on how to keep your relationship hot and healthy at www.AliciaMunoz.com.

CPSIA information can be obtained
at www.ICGtesting.com
Printed in the USA
LVHW050418230919
631856LV00001B/1/P

9 781641 521826